# BIBLICAL ECONOMICS

*Economic Myths versus Biblical Values*

**Robert L. White**

**University Press of America,® Inc.**
**Lanham · Boulder · New York · Toronto · Oxford**

4501 Forbes Boulevard
Suite 200
Lanham, Maryland 20706
UPA Acquisitions Department (301) 459-3366

PO Box 317
Oxford
OX2 9RU, UK


Printed in the United States of America
British Library Cataloging in Publication Information Available

Library of Congress Control Number: 2006921613
ISBN-13: 978-0-7618-3444-1 (paperback : alk. paper)
ISBN-10: 0-7618-3444-3 (paperback : alk. paper)

∞™ The paper used in this publication meets the minimum requirements of American National Standard for Information Sciences—Permanence of Paper for Printed Library Materials, ANSI Z39.48—1984

# CONTENTS

# PREFACE

This book is written to encourage preachers, teachers, and all who would advocate and work for greater social justice in our world, to challenge today's prevailing economic ideology that promotes greed and consumerism over the common good. This book views today's complex national and global economic issues through the lens of biblical faith. The main premise is that biblical values are the foundation of a just global economy. Although Jesus spoke considerably more about money and possessions than any other subject, there are relatively few congregations engaged in dialog and advocacy concerning the crucial public policies that impact our shared global future. Is it because any attempt to question or challenge the "free-market" ideology that elevates self-interest over the good of the community is met with a vitriolic defense of the conservative economic agenda, echoing its ideologues who saturate the print and broadcast media 24/7?

This book provides a thorough critique of the neoclassical economic theory that has been adopted as a pillar of conservative ideology, characterized by a number of myths, and resulting in policies that have led to extreme inequalities and lack of justice in our world. The focus of the book is about restoring a balance between a highly productive economy and the plethora of unfulfilled vital human needs, including high levels of poverty, persistently high unemployment for some segments of the population, and unmet human needs in housing, education, and health care. The book confronts economic myths with economic realities and the values inherent in the Judeo-Christian faith. The six myths deal with the individual versus the common good; resource exploitation versus environmental preservation; economic scarcity versus God's abundance; more-is-better versus the quality of life; determinism versus grace; and privatization versus stewardship.

# ACKNOWLEDGMENTS

The genesis of this work was my master's thesis at Union Theological Seminary in New York. I am indebted to Union Seminary for the opportunity to study there and be inspired by its great professors, such as Dr. James A. Forbes, Jr, who taught and preached biblical justice. I was also privileged to be at Union during the pastorate of the Rev. William Sloan Coffin at the adjacent Riverside Church. Dr. Forbes then succeeded Dr. Coffin as pastor of Riverside Church in 1988. The atmosphere of intellectual openness and theological relevance (in the tradition of Reinhold Niebuhr) allowed me to do research combining my work as an economist along with my theological study. The fruition of which is this book—honed by years of additional learning in serving as pastor of several congregations.

I dedicate this book to my wife Frances for her encouragement and patience at my many hours of being AWOL from family responsibilities while seemingly grafted to the computer, scrunching and shaping sources and snippets of information that evolved into the pages of this book. Without her enduring support this work would not have been possible.

I am also grateful for the assistance of Dr. H. Roy Kaplan, associate professor at the University of South Florida and formerly the executive director of The National Conference for Community and Justice for the Tampa Bay area, for his encouragement and helpful comments on the text. My grateful thanks also to my editor, Tammy Jaycox Kaplan, whose tireless efforts greatly helped to make this publication a reality. Any errors, commissions or omissions, are solely the responsibility of the author.

# 1

## A CONTEST OF PROPHETS

Whenever a preacher stands before the assembly, and attempts to proclaim a word from God as revealed in biblical texts, it is as formidable a challenge as when Elijah contended with 450 prophets of Baal and then some (I Kings 18). It is a contest between the values inherent in biblical texts and the myriad of spin-doctors saturating the print and broadcast media 24/7. This oft-cited "cultural wars" reflects two very different theologies—on one side the biblical faith, on the other the voices of consumerism and its idol, the "free-market" economy.

*Overview*

While we live in an age where heretics are no longer burned at the stake, speakers who would publicly attempt to challenge and demythologize the "free-market" economy would probably find themselves deep in controversy. Nevertheless, the purpose of this book is a reveille and call to challenge the idols and prophets of consumerism and greed. This book is for preachers, teachers, and all who would advocate and work for greater social justice in our world. This book views today's complex global and national economic trends through the lens of biblical faith. The main premise is that biblical values are the foundations of a just economy. This book presents an overall framework in which to discuss the tensions between biblical values and economic policies. It encourages the reader to begin to gather information and resources dealing with today's complex economic issues, and to analyze and interpret these economic issues within the perspective of biblical values.

Jesus spoke considerably more about money and possessions than any other subject. This book takes up that emphasis, encouraging both clergy and laity to advocate the biblical values that address human needs and the controversial social problems of our time. Religious congregations and community organizations should be as much involved in public policy formulation as the political, financial and business sectors. This dialogue and debate about our shared global future is so urgent and important that it must include the widest possible interests and perspectives.

This book does not advocate an alternative economic system as a cure or replacement of our present market-based economic system. The book does, however, set forth a critique of the values upon which our present economic *policies* are based. An alternative set of values is set forth—values based on biblical principles concerned with justice, equity, and fairness. This book argues that economic theory has become an ideology, reflected in a number of myths—myths supportive of policies which have led to extreme inequalities and lack of justice in several major areas, (e.g., high levels of poverty, persistently high unemployment and underemployment for some segments of our citizens, unmet human needs in housing, education, and health care). The focus of this book is about restoring a balance between a highly productive economy and the plethora of unfulfilled vital human needs in our world. It confronts economic myths with economic realities, and the values inherent in the Judeo-Christian scriptures.

*The Prophetic Task*

From ancient times, the role of a prophet is to bring critical standards of thought to the confusion and anxiety of his/her contemporary world; to question society's basic assumptions and presuppositions; and to offer a new vision of reality that offers an alternative to the prevailing personal and national self-interests. The prophet's challenge to the status quo is that reality is not necessarily the way the powers-that-be say so. The prophetic task today—challenging the parochial, national self-interest world view—is crucial and imminent in today's religion-embracing political climate, and our culture-embracing religious organizations.

The story of the prophet Elijah appears abruptly, like the abrasive troublemaker himself, in the book of First Kings, invading the secretive and corrupt royal court. The situation we find in this story is the hardship of an economic recession. A severe drought results in famine throughout Samaria. The government is beginning to look incompetent and unreliable. The inability of the government to deliver prosperity is beginning to raise questions about its authority and legitimacy. Instead the administration's economic policy further impoverishes the people. The question raised in the Elijah episode is whom do we trust—self-serving, political-promoting earthly powers—or God? The Elijah story is about how the hopeless cycle of need and poverty is broken by God's intervention. The prophetic ministry to which Elijah is called unmasks the false claims of the powers-that-be and offers a new possibility that arises out of and surpasses the drought-stricken world.[1]

When God decides it's time for the drought to end, Elijah is sent as messenger to proclaim to King Ahab that it is God who will send the rain. Yet Ahab does not understand. Ahab thinks that Baal, an idol believed to be the source of fertility and prosperity, characterizes the divine nature. So the question is posed who will send the rain, the idol Baal or the divinity as proclaimed by Elijah? Elijah condemns Ahab for not esteeming and acknowledging the God whom Elijah represented, a very different kind of unconstrained, uncontained, unpredictable, divinity.

To settle the competing claims about the nature of the true God, Elijah issues a challenge to the "four hundred fifty prophets of Baal and the four hundred prophets of Asherah" (both idols from the homeland of Jezebel, Ahab's wife). This contest, says Elijah to the people, will render a verdict: "If the Lord is God, follow him; but if Baal, then follow him," (I Kings 18:21b). The contest will reveal by which divine nature the drought will be ended, and to whom the future can be reliably entrusted. The contest will be a kind of cosmic Olympics to see how a divine blessing will be received—from a state-sponsored divinity, or from a divinity who is beyond human manipulation by public relations techniques or politics. The contest begins with the worshipers of Baal. From morning until afternoon they bounce and genuflect around the altar trying to win the favor of Baal; but there is "no voice, no answer, and no response," (I Kings 18:29). No fire rains down. Elijah sarcastically ridicules the ineffectiveness of their futile actions and misplaced trust.

Then it is Elijah's turn. He calls the people together and prepares for worship by repairing and reestablishing the divine altar. Digging a trench around the altar, he places a customary offering of seed and a slaughtered bull in the trench and thoroughly drenches it with water. Then Elijah calls on the divine and the fire fell from the sky "and consumed the burnt offering, the wood, the stones, and the dust, and even licked up the water that was in the trench. When all the people saw this, they fell on their faces and said, 'The Lord indeed is God; the Lord indeed is God'" (I Kings 18:38-39). Ever since, discerning the true nature of God from idolatry has been a challenge to people of faith.

We see from ancient times, prosperity and economic concerns were very much a part of religion. The official religious priests had a theory of what was the source of their society's economic prosperity. The prophets from Moses to Jesus had much to say about a different and other source of prosperity. Moses condemned the worship of the golden calf and Jesus overturned the tables of the temple moneychangers for their misplaced allegiance.

Idolatry has continued to be a problem for humans. In the Third Century, church theologian Origen preached passionately about the dangers of greed:

> God . . . knows that what a man loves with all his heart and soul and might—this for him is God. Let each one of us now examine himself and silently in his own heart decide which is the flame of love that chiefly and above all else is afire within him, which is the passion that he finds he cherishes more keenly than all others . . . Whatsoever it is that weighs the heaviest in the balance of your affection, that for you is God. But I fear that with very many the love of gold will turn the scale, that down will come the weight of covetousness lying heavy in the balance.[2]

This tension between scriptural values and the human desire for acquisitiveness has continued throughout the centuries. From the time of the Industrial Revolution, economic theory has become the theology of those who see economic growth as humankind's savior from poverty and misery. This has continued ever since with religion increasingly being the handmaiden of economics, as the church over the centuries has found mutual interest in allying itself with the economic powers-that-be.

Fortunately, there have arisen prophetic voices critical of the collusion between religion and economics. In the mid-19th century Washington Gladden, pastor of the First Congregational Church of Columbus, Ohio, often explored in his sermons the hazards of how money had become the true "religion of the multitude." The worship of "mammon," said Gladden, permeates American culture. The idolatry power of money affects us in obvious and subtle ways. It increasingly adds to our anxieties about our future—jobs, family needs, healthcare and retirement costs. For Gladden this spiritual warfare between faith and the god-like power of money was an issue for each believer, not just the "robber barons" of the day.[3]

More recently management guru Peter Drucker has also expressed the fanatical nature of materialism in a consumer-centered America.

> I have serious reservations about capitalism as a system because it idolizes economics as the be-all and end-all of life. It is one-dimensional; in short, whole dimensions of what it means to be a human being and treated as one are not incorporated into the economic calculus of capitalism. For such a myopic system to dominate other aspects of life is not good for any society.[4]

Owing to its success over the last several hundred years, there is a strongly founded belief in the "free-market" economy. Upon what is this belief based? It is a long-established historical record that the market system is the source of increasing prosperity for most people in the advanced industrialized countries. Market competition promotes specialization and technological innovation that are inducements for accelerated economic growth. With economic growth comes rising living standards and greater choices of goods and services. Yet, in a market-based economic system capital and financial assets tend to accumulate in greater and greater proportions at the top of the economic scale. Historically, the role of the federal government is to legislate policies for a fairer distribution of income, and to protect the health and security of all persons. In major industrial sectors, like banking and financial securities, the tendencies for abusive and illegal business practices have been constrained by government oversight and regulation.

In recent times, however, as a result of a more extreme free-market ideology, the economy is increasingly less regulated by government oversight. There is less regulation of polluting industries and increasing income inequality. Advocates of free-trade support a global market system that extends itself around the world, unregulated, unhindered, and unconstrained by any external influences. There have been recurrent reports of corporations exploiting and trampling over the human and civil rights of the people in Third World countries. Additionally, many voices in the Third World are increasingly skeptical as to whether the free-market system, which has created prosperity for most of the people in developed countries, will be able to bring prosperity to the half of the world's population that is struggling to subsist on two dollars or less a day. Moreover the growing evidence of intergenerational poverty and the stagnation of incomes for the majority of persons in the United States raises new questions about the fairness of the prevailing free-market economic policies.

The competitive market economy does produce efficiency. Few would question the assertion that the economy of the United States is the most productive and efficient in the world. The crucial questions concern justice issues related to income distribution—how equitably the wealth of this great productivity is shared among all its economic stakeholders and how prosperity in the United States and other developed nations impact the economic welfare of those in the Third World (formerly referred to as "less-developed countries").

# 2

# STATING THE PROBLEM AND ITS CRITIQUE

Present day orthodox economic theory is based on the thinking of Scottish Enlightenment philosopher Adam Smith. In his book *An Inquiry Into the Nature and Causes of the Wealth of Nations* (1776), Smith put forth a highly abstract economic model. At the center of the model is the self-interested individual who lives in a highly abstract, simplistic world, unlike the complex and multidimensional planet that we inhabit. According to this theory, the economy works best when left to itself (denoted by the French term *laissez-faire*) so that individuals are free to pursue their own self-interests. It is as though there is an "invisible hand" at work. Government interference can only hamper this positive working of the market. Competition leads investors to supply what is most wanted and keeps the prices as low as possible. Economic policies of *laissez-faire* are prescribed within each country, and free trade (eliminating barriers to trade) between countries are strongly advocated from this orthodox economic perspective.

In the simple textbook model of a pure and perfectly competitive market, the economy will automatically achieve the state of greatest efficiency, a very special and technical definition. This assertion that competitive free-markets will efficiently produce goods and services at the lowest possible price, and compensate labor and other factors of production, rests on a highly restrictive set of assumptions. Given these highly restrictive assumptions (i.e., perfect knowledge on the part of all participants, no barriers to entry for new market competitors, each person's consumption of goods and services does not effect anyone else's, there are no negative effects like pollution, all factors of production are perfectly mobile, there is full employment of all resources, and all natural resources are assumed to be unlimited, et. al.), then the model results in an optimal state of economic efficiency through the operation of a freely competitive market. The technical economic term for this is the Pareto Optimum (Vilfredo Pareto 1848-

1923)—no individual can be made better off without making some other individual worse off.

These conclusions are technically valid only in the abstract world of an eco nomics textbook. For in the real world most of the assumptions do not hold. In the real world everyone does not have accurate knowledge and information about all markets. There are barriers to entry (i.e., the huge capital costs required to start up a new automobile or aircraft manufacturer). There are external effects like pollution and environmental destruction. There is monopoly power distorting "free" markets, and there are unemployed and underemployed resources and workers—to name just a few contradictions to the assumptions of the orthodox economic model.

Within orthodox economics, however, there is recognition of the inconsistency and contradictions of these unrealistic assumptions of the textbook model. Therefore, according to the second-best theory in economics, in the real world where the restrictive assumptions of the textbook model do not hold, there can be no valid presumption that a market economy will actually achieve the desired economic results as purported by the textbook model. According to the second-best theory, being somewhere close to the goal of maximization does not permit one to assume that policies based on the maximization model would be valid and effective. Where the assumptions of the perfect competition model do not hold, then policy recommendations have to be made in an environment of uncertainty and not of economic determinism. Second-best policies are targeted to achieve a positive economic result in a complex and ambiguous economic environment where automatic and predetermined results can no longer be assumed.[5]

Unlike the other social sciences, neoclassical economics has a theory of what "ought to be." Unfortunately, real world empirical evidence has had little impact on this "ought to be" world. Increasingly the discipline of economics fails to explain the credibility gap between theory and the way the world's economy really works. This disconnect between formal economic theory and the real world is even greater than most economists are willing to admit. Two economists, Deidre McCloskey and Stephen Ziliak, have found that a great majority of the research articles published over the last two decades in the *American Economic Review* have failed to distinguish between what is economically significant versus what is statistically significant. Blinded by statistical wizardry many economists fail to ask whether their findings matter.[6]

The second-best case for collective action (including government involvement) in the economy where the market system cannot automatically result in economy-wide efficiency has been developed by economic theorists in the field of public finance.[7] According to this theory, the case for government involvement in the economy is justified under conditions in which:

1. The public needs to be protected from exploitation that would result from a pure *laissez-faire* system (i.e., child labor laws).
2. Public goods and services have to be provided. Where there are goods and services whose consumption and costs cannot be charged to the specific users of those goods and services, then there is no market incentive for any firm to supply costly goods for free. So, such public goods as highways, lighthouses, national defense, parks, scientific research and knowledge, flood control, etc., need to be provided by a government entity or some other form of collective organization.
3. There are consumption and production externalities with positive or negative effects. Production of some goods has consequences that are not limited to those who choose to engage in them. For example, air pollution resulting from a coal-burning power plant effects persons far beyond the customers served by that electric utility.
4. Natural monopolies exist, i.e., public utilities like transmission lines or projects like the Hoover Dam, where the capital costs and risks are so huge that they exceed private market capacity to finance them.
5. Economic stabilization is required to avoid severe recessions and depressions and to control inflation.
6. An acceptable rate of economic growth is desired, for instance, to promote full employment. Another consideration might be whether the rate of economic growth is ecologically sustainable.
7. To meet social need, certain income redistribution objectives are required. This important point is that even if maximum efficiency could be achieved in the real world through a perfectly competitive market, the resulting income distribution may not be what society considers fair or equitable. An economically efficient solution obtained through the markets could hypothetically result in one percent of the population owning 99 percent of the resources—unfair, but (hypothetically) in a strictly technical sense, efficient.

It is just such situations and conditions that government policies or voluntary forms of collective action (i.e., homeowners' associations and civic and non-profit organizations) attempt to achieve a positive economic result in a complex economic environment where all economic objectives cannot automatically be achieved by the market system alone. An example of a public policy to achieve a specific economic objective is local government land-use and public facilities planning. Comprehensive planners attempt to implement land-use policy to direct market forces to develop within designated areas to achieve a rational development pattern to benefit the entire community.

Free competition does produce economic efficiency. The problem is that the textbook case of the economy automatically achieving an idealized and illusory "optimality," if unfettered by outside influences, cannot be achieved in the real world. That is because all the conditions for this idealized (and idolized) optimality cannot hold in the real world.

As has been shown, there is no theoretical or empirical reason to expect all of society's economic objectives to be met systematically by the market. In other words, justice, equity, and fairness cannot be assumed to occur automatically, and therefore need to be intentional goals and objectives in the realm of public policy. In general, as many policy instruments are needed as there are policy targets.[8]

Indeed, since there are non-market, non-competitive economic arrangements in our economy besides free competition, the question needs to be asked whose interests are being served by these non-market arrangements? Single-source defense contracting, for instance, is a non-market activity. Too often, the ideology of perfect competition is used as an ideological smokescreen to disguise the actual operation of non-market arrangements. Just as these other non-market objectives are pursued by the economy, the ends of justice and equality needs to be objectified and pursued as specific policy goals. As philosopher John Rawls has affirmed (and echoed by a number of religious observers in recent years), social justice requires that a just society be characterized by a continual improvement in the prospects of the least advantaged.[9]

From this perspective, it is the primary assertion of this book that orthodox economic theory, as described above, functions as a smoke screen to hide certain social policies in the guise of "free-market capitalism." The so-called theory of market economics masks a defense of the status quo that works against solving the complex problems of community and national life. The working of the market economy over the last 20 years has resulted in increasing inequalities, persistent poverty, chronic unemployment, and more persons without health insurance. Instead of these disparities being ameliorated by government, these problems have been exacerbated by tax cuts for the wealthy, and the resulting huge budget deficits. Since 2001, the public trust has been violated, the public treasury raided, and some fear an intensive governmental assault has been launched on public education, Social Security, and Medicare. Just as we need citizen participation in community planning, we need better public involvement in advocating and achieving better economic policy for justice and fairness.

# 3

# MYTH #1: INDIVIDUALISM VERSUS INTERDEPENDENCE

The core assumption of the theory, practice, and ideology of economics is a particular and unique concept of the individual. This highly abstract concept is in polar contradiction to both our biblical faith and the world in which we live. As was stated in the previous section, the sole motivation of the economic person is self-interest. Another characteristic of this highly abstract, purely economic being is insatiability, that is, more is always better. People always want more of everything and our greed is only constrained by a budget. Yet, on the contrary, we know that humans are capable of great compassion, generosity (charity and philanthropy), self-denial, and sacrifice.

*Neighborhood Economics*

Orthodox economic theory requires many highly restrictive assumptions. One restrictive and unrealistic assumption essentially states that one consumer's choices of goods and services are independent of another person's consumer choices. Each individual makes his or her economic decisions totally independent of other peoples' economic decisions.

We know that this is neither true, nor in the community's best interest. We are increasingly aware that one person's consumption of scarce resources *does* have a "neighborhood" or community-wide effect. For example, a person may want to run the biggest urban armored personnel carrier on leaded, 98-octane gasoline. However, due to the resultant degrading of the air quality, this individual cannot do this ethically or legally. For the public good, legislation and regulations have restricted the kinds of gasoline that can be sold and consumed. Thus private goods often have side effects that have public/community impacts such as pollution and congestion. The public nature of private consumption is much wider than is generally recognized. In reality, we live in a highly interdependent world. One person's consumption does in a variety of complex interrelated ways affect other persons' welfare.

The following diagram graphically depicts this relationship:

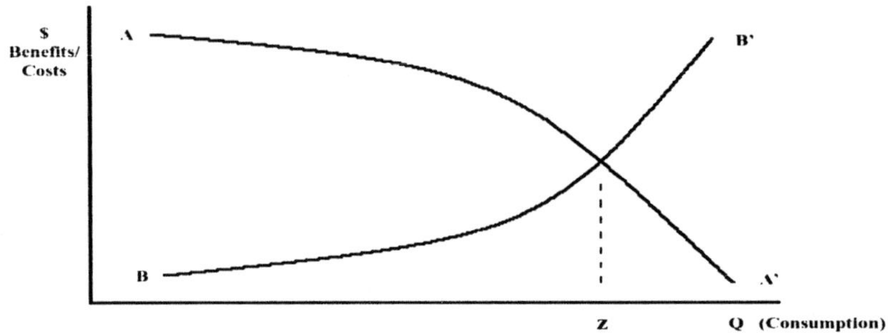


This figure shows a situation in which an activity of individual A generates negative impacts (externalities) on individual B. The marginal net benefits from A's activity are illustrated by the downward sloping line (AA'), reflecting decreasing marginal benefits to A (according to the "law of diminishing returns"—each unit consumed is incrementally less valued). The costs incurred by B resulting from A's activity are indicated by an upward sloping line (BB'), illustrating increasing incremental costs or damages to B as A's activity continues.

At activity levels up to Z, the marginal amount of B's damages is less than A's marginal net benefit. In the absence of regulation and in terms of a market-based solution, B cannot offer A enough to stop A's activity. At levels greater than Z, B's marginal damages exceed A's marginal net benefits, so gains from trade are possible because B is willing to pay A to restrict A's activity to level Z, an amount greater than the benefits A would receive by expanding activity beyond Z. The common good is served when A's gain is maximized while minimizing B's loss. In this example, this maximum is at point Z. (The situation becomes much more complex when it involves a city dumping sewage into a river—causing damages to many users downstream. If A's activity negatively effected 100 Bs, there is the possibility of a considerable increase in the costs of negotiation and regulation.)

Of course, this is a simplistic example, and such a cost/benefit approach runs the danger of reducing human life to only monetary terms and treating humans as means rather than ends. Yet it illustrates the fundamental notion that the activity and gains of one person may have a negative effect and impose costs or damages on someone else, contrary to the free-market economic model. Also, there is the subjective problem of how to measure the costs and benefits to each party—what variables to measure and ascertaining how to measure these variables. Nevertheless, the diagram makes the point: no one is an island—and in society, often someone's gain is at someone else's expense.

The free-market economic model does not realistically describe the complexity of our economic system, which is a mix of the private and public sectors, providing goods and services in conjunction with both large and small businesses, stores, schools, hospitals, public utilities, and other economic organizations. In such a complex system, it is no wonder that there are alternative models of economic organization and production. The open-source model in the world of software has been suggested as a post-capitalist model in other areas such as medical research and pharmaceuticals. The open-source model refers to the practice of allowing many users to collaborate on the development of software by making its core program, or source code, available to everyone.

> By far the best-known example of open-source software is Linux, an operating system that is maintained by volunteers around the world, runs on everything from wristwatches to mainframes and now powers one in five of the world's server computers.[10]

Opponents of open source are commercial software vendors who jealously guard their source code so they can continue to earn fees and royalties for their products.

It is still far from certain whether the open-source model would work in other industries. Another question is whether open-sourcing would inspire innovation or stifle it. Nevertheless the success in some areas like software indicate that collective goodwill in pursuing common aims can result in developments and products for the greater good of all. The open-source approach is another example of cooperative mutual interests triumphing over private self-interest.

*Interdependence and Community*

The concept of the individual, upon which market economic theory is based, is foreign to our biblical faith. The values and behaviors set forth in the Bible are in the context of a highly interdependent community. From the biblical perspective, human beings from the beginning were not self-sufficient, but were dependent upon God, one another, and nature (the garden, animals, and all of creation). God had intended that humans would live in God's creation in harmony with all other living things and the natural environment.

One word that truly defines the human condition is *interdependence*. Interdependence means that all things that share space on this planet are interrelated. For instance, the problems of environmental pollution of the land, air, and water remind us that human well-being is very much dependent upon the health of our environment.

Interdependence is illustrated in the following example. Some years back, a clergyman in a large northeastern city was working to rehabilitate abandoned properties in the inner city. After many months of hard labor and the frustrations of battling the bureaucratic hurdles and obstacles thrown in front of him by an uncooperative city hall, he moved into one of the rehabilitated homes. Sometime later someone set a fire in an adjacent vacant property. To fight the fire in the dilapidated building, the firemen broke through his newly rehabilitated walls, demolishing a great deal of that for which he had labored so long. As a result of this loss, he wrote a poem with the refrain, "We all live in attached houses."

That is why all citizens are taxed for the provision of fire protection. No one can opt out of fire protection because if even one house is burning—all houses in that community are imperiled. That is why we have fire protection for an entire metropolitan region. Either we are all safe—or no one is safe. In an interdependent world, we have many mutual interests.

Fire is no respecter of persons. The raging infernos throughout the southwest in recent years of drought, and the widespread torching and destruction of our planet's rainforests are a grim reminder that we all live in attached houses—no matter how far away you are from your neighbor's house. The destruction and imperiling of the environment anywhere affects every resident on space station earth.

Likewise environmental problems, like saving our rainforests, teach us how interdependent life is on this planet. Issues of economic justice are interrelated to environmental justice. The people of Brazil, as are many in Third World countries, are burdened with the repayment of enormous debts which will probably further impoverish the country and result in more deaths from hunger and easily preventable diseases. Poverty pushes people out into the rainforests to try to find a minimal level of existence, which results in the further destruction of trees. So if something is not done to alleviate the poverty in countries like Brazil, the devastation of the rainforests will continue with increasing and cumulative effects on all of us—rich and poor countries alike.

The same argument for the high interdependence of life can be made for the case of health care. An individual's health is dependent upon the general level of community health. For instance, 50 years ago when an effective polio vaccine was available, vaccinations were provided to the general population at no cost to the individual. Taxes paid for the vaccinations for the majority of school age children. Polio could only have been eradicated if enough of the population was vaccinated.[11]

The divine concern and intent for social harmony in human community is also reflected in the concept of *covenant.* After God delivered the Hebrews out of bondage in Egypt, God initiated a covenant, or partnership, in which God and people were obligated to each other. These codes were not meant to be arbitrary prohibitions and limitations of life; indeed, it was these specific laws and codes that made community possible, protecting life and property and demanding respect for parents, spouses, neighbors, and family. As well, they promote a special concern for the vulnerable members of the community: widows, orphans, the poor, and refugees. Interdependence in the human community as set forth by the biblical concept of covenant directly implies that society be organized for the mutual benefit of all. The most disadvantaged, for instance, who could not provide or protect themselves were to be provided for and protected.[12] Traditional tribal societies know a simple truth: The survival and well being of the community depends ultimately upon the survival and well being of each person in the community. It is just as true today; we all live in a global village.

When the poor and powerless were not shown compassion and respect, God sent prophets like Amos to condemn the injustice, deceit, and exploitation

(Amos 8:4-8). In the face of growing inequalities, the prophets called the people to repent and to remember the right relationship to God and to their neighbor. As we read in Amos, *shalom* (peace) is dependent upon the crucial prerequisites of justice and righteousness. Justice and righteousness called for the widow, the orphan and the refugee to be helped, since they were at a disadvantage in caring for themselves. A century later, in a similar way, Jeremiah condemns Judah and the rich who builds his house by "unrighteousness, his upper rooms by injustice" (Jeremiah 22:13-17).[13] Righteousness referred to an atmosphere of right relations, with God and one another. Justice referred to specific acts of justice that would promote or restore these right relationships. Acts of justice support and restore healthy relationships in community. When righteousness and justice prevail, then *shalom*, or community-wide peace will naturally follow.[14]

In this prophetic tradition, Jesus took up the cause of the poor and powerless. He ministered to the widow, the children, the homeless, the hungry, and the oppressed. Furthermore, he said, that all nations would be judged by how they treated the hungry, thirsty, stranger, naked, sick, and the imprisoned (Matthew 25:31-46). The righteous are those who have met the demands of their fellow neighbors in community relationship.

Justice and righteousness are also the basic values upon which Jesus' Great Commandment stands (Matthew 22:34-40). When a lawyer asked Jesus which is the greatest commandment, Jesus responded quoting two verses from the Hebrew scriptures: "You shall love the Lord your God with all our heart, and with all your soul, and with all your might" (Deuteronomy 6:5); and "You shall love your neighbor as yourself" (Leviticus 19:18b). Jesus added his commentary, "On these two commandments hang all the law and the prophets" (Matthew 22:40). God calls his people to live peacefully and respectfully with each other in community. All are to partake together of the plenty or the scarcity that God and circumstances provide (Acts 4:32).

Another important biblical word reflecting our shared reality of interdependence is the word *compassion*, which according to its Latin roots literally means to suffer with. Whether through our own experience or through empathy, most of us know something about feeling exiled, lost, deserted, abandoned, neglected, in need, hungry, uprooted, or homeless. The test of a nation's capacity to be compassionate is how we treat the poorest in society, and those most in need. Every major world religion has some form of the Golden Rule, "In everything do to others as you would have them do to you," (Matthew 7:12). As Jesus revealed in the parable of the Good Samaritan (Luke 10:29-37), respect and care for neighbors is meant not just to be extended to those whom we feel are most like ourselves, but equally to unrecognized strangers as well. We are true to our biblical faith when we extend care and compassion to those who are in need. The ethic of compassion implied in the Golden Rule has to do with the question of in what kind of society do we want to live?

The letters of Paul the Apostle clearly reveal the social implication of justice and righteousness:

> The righteousness of God—given, received, and lived out—is not just a personal but also a corporate reality. It involves participation in a community of people who risk their own security by being *for* others whose histories may be radically different, who culturally, ethnically, economically, politically, and/or socially live on the other side of the tracks. Movement from the old dominion of death to the new dominion of life draws people into a strange fellowship where previously significant divisions no longer matter. To cling to these anachronistic barriers is to reject the demand that the gift of God's righteousness has made. Justification for Paul, then, implies social action in the broadest sense. It implicates the recipient in the cause of sisters and brothers of various circumstances who labor under the weight of oppression, affliction, and personal grief. The divine acquittal is received not by faith which may someday lead to a social concern (or may not) but by faith that *is* social concern, or to use Paul's word, "faith working through love" (Gal. 5:6).[15]

The First Century Christian community exemplified these attitudes and concerns. The members of this believing community "held all their possessions in common: and they sold their possessions and goods and distributed them to all as any had need." (Acts 2:44-45). The Corinthian church had a similar communal ethical commitment (2 Corinthians 8:1-15).

As part of God's creation, material possessions are good—gifts from God. What is warned against in both the Hebrew and Greek testaments is the covetous accumulation of wealth, especially if riches for the few mean deprivation for others. Wealth is denounced when it leads to indifference (Amos 6:4-6) or causes oppression (1 Samuel 12:1-4), or when it is idolatrous (Matthew 6:24).

Also, since the Creator has fashioned humankind in the image of God (Genesis 1:27), an economic system that is faithful to God must be based on care and respect for every person. It is somewhat paradoxical that while free-market economic theory speaks of human beings as "sovereign" consumers—emphasizing the importance of individual consumer choices—yet, on the production side, the human being is demoted to only another economic factor of production (labor), along with the other factors, (i.e., capital, land and resources). When human beings are treated like inanimate "factors of production," their divinely intended status as persons in the image of God is violated. Social justice requires that there be a respect for the equal worth of all members within human society.

In striving to free ourselves from the myth of the automatic benevolence of the "free-market," we may be able to see a greater and grander truth on a more global and universal scale. The communities from biblical times understood on a deep level that all things do work for the good, and "You reap what you sow." The communities from biblical times understood that righteousness brought its own rewards—*shalom* and prosperity. Unrighteousness met another kind of judgment—destruction and the loss of the land. Over the course of history has not the unrighteousness of every empire been a major underlying cause of that empire's demise? Is not there a judgment in this life on both the righteous and the unrighteous?

As Fred Hirsch has pointed out, "A system that depends for its success on a heritage that it undermines cannot be sustained on the record of its bountiful fruits."[16] In this Hirsch refers to the emphasis on economic individualism that is undermining the religious values and virtues upon which capitalism has thrived—shared values, mutual interests, and cooperation. Economic justice must focus on the public nature of society as a whole, and the collective nature of the economy. From this perspective the private market cannot, by itself, provide for all these considerations.

# 4

## Myth #2: ECONOMIC EXPLOITATION VERSUS EARTH-KEEPING ECOLOGY

The impressionist artist Paul Gauguin while in Tahiti painted one of his greatest masterpieces, "From where do we come? What are we? Where are we going?" Juxtaposed against the surreal background of an enchantingly primitive and pristine paradise, we see people going about their everyday lives. Yet the title implies that these are the basic questions that all humans will ask at one time or another. Why do we reflect on such questions?

*Common Ground*

Perhaps a partial answer to these questions is offered by one of the great spiritual writers of our time, Carlo Carretto, who has referred to creation as a parable of God.[17] That is, we humans see the hand of God in the harmony and beauty of everything in creation. God's handprint is on everything from the delicate rose petal to the brilliant sunset; every living, and natural thing suggests a Creator. People in every time and place seek to understand how we and all of nature were created. So from time to time it is only natural that we contemplate the origins of all life.

The Hebrew Bible's account (Genesis chapters 1 and 2), scholars tell us, was actually written during Israel's Exile, in the 6th Century B.C.E. (Before the Common Era). The stories existed in oral form for centuries before they were put in written form. Why at the time of the Exile was it necessary to record these stories in writing? When the Israelites were in Babylon, they heard all about the Babylonian gods, especially Baal, the god of fertility and prosperity. So they needed to tell the truth about the divinity whom they experienced to be the real Creator of life: "The earth is the Lord's and all the fullness thereof, the world and all who dwell therein" (Psalm 24:1).

Even today, belief in a god of prosperity is still prevalent. Today's prosperity "theology" is called the theory of "free-market" economics. It is the view of this book that belief in this god of prosperity and its theology is an alternative to and different from the divine nature as revealed in the Bible, both the Hebrew and Christian scriptures.

The persons who were inspired to shape these verses of the Creation story into the book of Genesis were writing in a pre-scientific age. So we should think of these verses more like poetry rather than an alternative to scientific explanations of the origin of the universe. Yet, however primitive this poetry may be, it is marvelous how the writer understands all of creation to be a vital and abundant living system in which all things are related, created by God out of the formless chaos of nonexistence.

The creation story in Genesis suggests the image of a mobile, with all its parts connected in an interdependent system. The creation story tells us that we are part of creation, not separate from it. We are made of the same stuff as everything else—everything has emerged according to God's master plan from chaos created only by God's word.

As the astronomer Timothy Ferris has said,

> When we look at subatomic particles, and when we look at the stars and galaxies, we see evidence from every direction that the universe is all of a piece, and that it began as a single seed smaller than an atom . . . Every scrap of matter and energy in our blood and bones and in the synapses of our thoughts, can trace its lineage back to the origin of the universe. The natural laws that fragmented and multiplied as the young universe expanded and cooled continue to operate today in the beating of our hearts, as well as in the trajectories of the stars . . . Our thoughts and feelings after all, are part of the universe too.[18]

When God calls upon the human to take care of the garden and "to till it and keep it" (Genesis 2:15), we should think of earth-keeping rather than dominance and exploitation. Dominance leads to violence and war with nature. Perhaps the key word is *responsibility*. Responsibility literally means to be able to respond. When we respond to the rest of creation we are responsible for it. When we move our part of creation, it affects everything else. Scientists who study chaos theory can prove a theorem that states that when a butterfly flaps it wings in Beijing, it affects the weather everywhere in the world. Responsibility also implies that everything else responds to the individual's actions. So responsibility means affecting the environment in such a way that we realize it will have an effect on everything else, not only now but also for generations to come. An African proverb says, "The world was not left to us by our parents, it was lent to us by our children."

The Apostle Paul had a way of speaking about this interdependent *responsibility.* Paul said, "for you reap whatever you sow" (Galatians 6:7b). How we affect life, will be the way that life responds to us. How we treat God's creation, including our sisters and brothers, will determine our future well-being. What we give will be the measure of what we receive. Everything is interrelated—it's all about responsibility.

How we respond today to our environment will determine what kind of future our children and grandchildren will have. Hopefully we are not repeating the "Tragedy of the Commons." In medieval England, many villages were built around a plot of common grazing land. Frequently that common land was over-grazed as population grew and people tried to maximize their family wealth with more livestock. Putting more animals in to graze benefited each family in the short term. Yet, doing so eventually ruined the space for all. So common resources, without management and controls, almost always will be exhausted or abused.[19] The issue today is the carrying capacity of "the commons" which has become the whole planet. For example, in the United States and other industrialized countries there are now frequent advisories warning the public about the dangers of eating fish due to the high levels of mercury concentrated in the fish.

Over the last several years there is increasing concern about global warming. The effects have been even greater on the North and South Poles. While the average temperature of the earth has only risen by one degree Fahrenheit, over the past 100 years, the temperature at the Poles has increased four degrees. Research in Canada's Hudson Bay has shown that the ice season has been shortened by about two and a half weeks, limiting the time polar bears have to prey on seals for sustenance. So they are not as fat, and are not coming through the winter as well. Their lives and future are endangered. *Our* common resources are endangered.

Surging oil prices since 1973 and growing concerns about air pollution and cutting greenhouse gases produced by burning fossil fuels have spurred efforts around the world to improve energy efficiency. Unfortunately, the United States, the world's largest energy consumer, has lagged behind. Japan, France and Germany consume 50 percent less energy per capita than does the United States. In Japan, energy consciousness has probably reached the highest level of any country. Although Japan's industrial production has tripled since 1973, its energy consumption has remained nearly flat. Japan is investing billions of dollars to reduce its emission of global warming gases by the year 2012 to six percent below the 1990 level. Higher fuel efficiencies are being achieved in home appliances, building materials, hybrid automobiles, and by using alternative technologies like solar energy and fuel cells. Japan, with a population of only 44 percent that of the United States, produces more electricity from photovoltaic solar panels than the combined total of the two next biggest consumers, Germany and the United States.[20]

While the United States comprises only five percent of the world's population, we are responsible for about 20 percent of the "greenhouse" gases like carbon dioxide that result in great quantity from the burning of fossil fuels. The issue of the need to reduce the emission of these gases shows how everything is related in an interdependent world. Making peace with the environment in the case of greenhouse gases also goes with making peace in the world. Prospects for peace in the Middle East would surely improve if the United States decided to stop our over dependence on cheap oil imports from that part of the world. When will it be the patriotic as well as the environmentally enlightened thing to do to trade in a gas-guzzling SUV for a fuel-efficient hybrid vehicle?

For tens of thousands of years humans created no problems for the natural environment. From the beginnings of human society, the native people have shared resources held in common—like rain forests, prairies, and streams. These native people live as if in large extended families, sharing work, resources, and mutual support. Unfortunately, modern humans have taken the environment for granted; believing that the earth's land, water, and air were so vast and resilient that people could never do the environment serious harm. Since the beginning of the Industrial Revolution, business and industry have regarded the environment as an almost unlimited source of energy and raw materials, and a free dumping ground. The results of the past two centuries of economic activity have been air pollution, water pollution, acid rain, global warming, and the accumulation of toxic and hazardous wastes. The ozone layer, which shields us from the sun's ultraviolet rays, has been weakened and damaged.

It has been widely repeated since the beginning of our era of increased environmental awareness that in order to bring everyone on the planet to the same high-consumption living standard as the average person in North America would require four or five more Earths. Yet the developing countries, mired in poverty and debt, are being asked to take expensive steps to avoid the disastrous environmental path already followed by the developed countries.

The destruction of the environment over decades has created one ecological catastrophe after another. The pollution of our air, land, oceans, lakes, rivers and streams has occurred over decades. As documented in a recent newspaper, here is a typical example of economic exploitation of the environment:

> The Fenholloway River teemed with redfish and mullet. Fishermen gathered oysters and crabs where the river emptied into the Gulf of Mexico, 50 miles south of Tallahassee.
>
> Fed by a stream, the river water was bottled and sold as Fenhollowway Sulphur Water, a cure for arthritis and kidney problems.
>
> Change came in 1947, when Proctor & Gamble called on Taylor County. P&G wanted to build a pulp plant and make the river its toilet, flushing its waste out to the gulf. Local politicians, envisioning jobs and capital, pronounced this a fine idea.
>
> Lobbyists went to work. The bill they offered the legislature designated the Fenholloway an "industrial river." Any manufacturing or industrial plant in Taylor county, it said, "is hereby empowered to discharge and deposit sewage, industrial and chemical wastes and effluents, or any of them, into the waters of the Fenholloway river and the waters of the Gulf of Mexico into which said river flows."
>
> The House passed it April 22, 1947, the Senate the next day. Votes in both chambers were unanimous. The legacy of those votes is a river the color of Coca Cola, swathed with white scum. The fish are gone, the oxygen choked

from the waters.

> "The Fenholloway stinks," a woman from Perry described it 22 years back. "And if the wind is from the east, especially if it's a damp or foggy day, you'd think a skunk had died under the porch."
>
> Despite cleanup efforts, the Fenholloway still smells like rotten cabbage.[21]

Since the first Earth Day in 1970, it has taken years of persevering hard and diligent work to gain environmental legislation to begin to repair the cumulative environmental damage of the last century. In the last couple of years some of the most important environment-saving legislation has been undone. The Clean Air Act passed by Congress in 1970 required industrial polluters to clean up their operations. The law forced newly built power plants and large factories to minimize their emissions of harmful pollutants like sulfur dioxide and lead. Congress updated the act in 1977 to apply to old plants that were being renovated or undergoing major overhauls.[22]

For over 20 years the electric industry complained about and lobbied against most of the clean air regulations, while at the same time many people in the vicinity of power plants were experiencing serious health problems. Power plants spew dozens of chemicals into the air; among the most harmful are nitrogen oxides, sulfur dioxide and mercury. Mercury is a highly toxic chemical that is emitted as a vapor when coal is burned. It has been found to cause brain disorders in unborn and young children. Warnings have been issued about the high levels of mercury in most fish like swordfish and tuna. Coal-fired plants account for 40 percent of the mercury. Pollution-controlling scrubbers can cut emissions up to 95 percent.

In November 1999 the U.S. Environmental Protection Agency (EPA) working through the Justice Department announced lawsuits against seven electric utility companies in the Midwest and South, charging that their power plants had been illegally releasing enormous amount of pollutants, in some cases for 20 years or more. The short version of the story is that after the 2000 elections these lawsuits were not pursued, and the regulations of the Clean Air Act pertaining to power plants were not enforced, and in some areas the regulations were reversed by means of regulatory changes and bureaucratic directives. The Bush Administration proposed new standards for mercury emission that would permit the release of as much as seven times as much mercury as current law allows. According to EPA staff estimates, the old regulations would have led to a 90 percent reduction in power-plant mercury emissions by 2008. The revised regulations would lead to a 70 percent reduction by 2018 or longer. According to

James K. Hammitt of the Harvard Center for Risk Analysis, the revised EPA policies allowing higher mercury emissions are based on faulty cost-benefit analysis that underestimates the negative human health impacts and the resultant higher costs for millions of affected people.[23]

The environmental damage, caused in this generation and past generations will be paid for by future generations. In this way, pollution is like the huge federal budget deficit—the costs incurred today will have to be born by future generations, generation after generation. Children are already suffering from increased levels of pollution. The incidence of asthma is nearly epidemic. At the end of 2004, the U.S. Environmental Protection Agency identified 224 counties in 20 states that do not meet the new clean air standards designed to protect against one of the most harmful pollutants, microscopic soot. So we must care about our environment and all its resources if we care about future generations—those who will be paying for the environmental costs we are incurring today.

What we need is a "sustainable economy" for the entire planet that will both supply human needs and protect the environment. According to ethicist Daniel Maguire, if people representing all the religions in the world got together they would find common ground on how to save the world from ecological destruction. It is only through such a combined effort of all the peoples of faith that the planet can be saved. The native peoples of the world—all the Native Americans in North and South America, all the aboriginals throughout the Southern Hemispheres, all the tribal peoples of Africa seem to much more respect and have a closer relationship to the earth than do the peoples of the Western developed nations.[24]

The Native Americans, for instance, believe than human beings should act according to how our actions today will impact on the next generations—even to the seventh generation. As Chief Seattle said, "This we know: The earth does not belong to us, we belong to the earth. This we know: All things are connected like the blood, which unites one family. All things are connected."[25] We could learn much from native peoples about how to live peacefully with our natural environment.

The Buddhists, Chinese, and Hindus have a deep sense of balance and harmony in life, and with all living things. We could learn much from them about how to live in balance and harmony with nature and each other. The Buddhists speak about the practice of "mindfulness" which means a heightened sense of awareness—of ourselves, life, and all living things.

Three of the great religions of the world Judaism, Islam, and Christianity all have a common ancestor, Abraham. They also have a strong sense of prophetic justice—what to do about great economic imbalance in a world where so many do not have enough and a relative few have an overabundance. Prophetic faith also leads us to care for and maintain the health of our God-given environment.

Jesus who lived in the traditional society of the ancient world was fully attuned to nature. Life was dependent upon the seasons—and each season's accordant rainfall, sunshine, and other factors affecting the planting, cultivation, and harvesting of crops. No wonder Jesus used various parables and figures of speech referencing the natural environment. Jesus spoke about seeds growing into large bushes as a metaphor for the kingdom of God. When teaching about our relation to the material world, he advised us to consider the birds and lilies (Matthew 6:25-34; Luke 12:22-31).

Christians believe that God through Christ entered anew into God's own creation. If God in Christ is reconciling the world, then Christ is also healing and restoring the relationships and harmony of nature broken by human greed and selfishness. In this way Christ is also reconciling the brokenness of humans and their environment. Someone has referred to the kingdom of God as God's creation healed and restored. It is in this spirit that most modern New Testament scholars and theologians interpret the words of Jesus as not so much preparing for an eternal life hereafter, but for service to the created world in the sure hope of the world's transformation at the time of God's final triumph. Through Jesus' teachings we have received a vision of God's intention to overcome all hostility and brokenness, and to bring healing and peace to all creation. As we await God's final triumph, we are to care for, nurture and sustain all of God's creation.

In the last chapters of the book of Revelation we read of the river of life and the tree of life that are in the new city from the heavenly realms. The "river of life" and the "tree of life" are good metaphors and images for the environment. We have been called to take care of the trees and rivers of life. From one of the religious writing of Judaism we read: "Just as you found trees which others had planted when you entered the land, so you should plant for your children. No one should say, 'I am old. How many more years will I live? Why should I be troubled for the sake of others?' Just as he found trees, he should add more by planting even if he is old."[26] Our lives are sustained by the trees and all the living and vital things in God's wondrous creation. We only have this one planet, and God has charged us to care for it. Let us take care of the trees and the whole God-given environment for the sake of our children, and their children, and their children . . . even to the seventh generation—so that hopefully that seventh generation who has lent us this earth to enjoy for awhile will not be disappointed by what we have done as stewards of the resources and the environment that they have entrusted to us.

*Regaining Lost Values*

Over the last decade, The Earth Charter resulted from the impetus for ecological, social, and economic justice as demanded by persons concerned about the environmental crises confronting humanity. At the 1992 United Nations Earth Summit at Rio de Janeiro, the idea was introduced that economic development must be sustainable—the negative impacts of economic activity must remain within the limits of the carrying capacity of the Earth's natural resources. The United States, however, blocked most of the significant actions that were proposed. (Just as a decade later the United States was the only industrialized nation not to sign the Kyoto Protocols that set limits on the emission of gases that damage the ozone layer and cause global warming.) Little if anything resulted from the Earth Summit. A group of private citizens working with Non-Governmental Organizations (NGOs) in numerous conferences and meetings from 1994 to 2000 took it upon themselves to draft a more meaningful document that would be a template for international environmental cooperation, resulting in March 2000 in the Earth Charter (see Appendix 1).

The broad-based ideas and principles that influenced the shaping of the Earth Charter include: new developments in international law and global ethics, new discoveries in cosmology, physics, and ecology. It also draws upon the wisdom of the world's religions and philosophies, and reflects the rising consciousness concerning human rights, democracy, racial and gender equality, disarmament and peace. The comprehensive values of the Earth Charter: interdependence for all life, the need for a sustainable planet, reverence for creation, respect for universal human rights, advocacy for economic and social justice, and promoting democratic and participatory societies, can be the foundation upon which to build a healthier and more peaceful world.

# 5

## MYTH #3: ECONOMIC SCARCITY VERSUS GOD'S ABUNDANCE

According to several recent economic studies, during the past three decades economic inequality has been increasing. The lion's share of the increase in national income is accumulating in the coffers of the top one percent of population. Conversely, the incomes of those in the middle have stagnated, and the bottom twenty percent of the population have seen their incomes decline. According to a 2005 analysis by the *New York Times*, the share of the nation's income earned by the top 0.1 percent (the top one-thousandth), those persons with average incomes of $3 million, has doubled since 1980. Their share rose to 7.4 percent in 2002, and in the year 2000 it exceeded 10 percent, a level last seen in the 1920s. The share of income earned by the top 10 percent was 44 percent. The share of income earned by the remaining 90 percent has fallen.[27] Wealth (net worth) like income, is concentrated at the top. According to the 2001 survey by the Federal Reserve Board, the top one percent of households' owned one-third of all financial and real assets. The next 9 percent of households owned about another third of all assets. The bottom 90 percent of all households held the remaining one-third of all wealth. The lowest 50 percent of the population (almost 150 million persons) owned only three percent of the total national wealth, while the nation's 400 wealthiest individuals ("Forbes 400") held over two percent of the nation's total net worth.[28]

*Increasing Inequality in the United States*

Since 2000, 4.3 million more persons fell below the poverty line, raising the total to about 36 million persons (or 12.5 percent of the population) who are living in poverty. Many experts think that the poverty definition should be revised substantially raising the total estimated number of poor. According to the U.S. Department of Agriculture, 12 million families (11 percent of the population) are "food insecure"—people either suffering from hunger or are relying on food assistance programs to avoid hunger.[29]

There are over 45 million persons with no health insurance something that should alarm even those who do have adequate health insurance. Beside the issue of care and compassion, we need to consider what happens when an epidemic hits. No one would be well for long, if there were sick people everywhere. A nation is only as healthy as all of its citizens. The United States, with so many of its citizens uninsured, expends a greater share of its gross domestic product (15 percent) on health care than do France or Canada (10 percent each)—both countries that provide health care insurance for all its citizens. While it is true that physicians' salaries are significantly higher in the United States than in Canada and France, the largest cost differential involves paperwork. According to a 2003 study in the New England Journal of medicine, administrative costs consume 31 cents out of every dollar spent on health care in the United States, compared to 17 cents in Canada.[30] The higher administrative costs are no doubt associated with the fragmented approach to providing health care in the United States compared to providing health care in a more unified national system—as is the case in every other industrialized county. Another benefit of a uniform system of national health care is that it allows for greater negotiating power on behalf of consumers. For example, Americans pay twice as much for prescription drugs as persons in other developed nations that benefit from collective bargaining with the pharmaceutical industry and health care providers.

While the rich have been getting richer and the poor poorer, tax rates have been drastically reduced for the top economic strata at a time when their incomes and been more than doubling. In the first 10 years when all the tax cuts enacted and proposed in the President's FY 2006 budget are fully effective, they will cost $2.5 trillion. More than 70 percent of the benefits would go to the 20 percent of taxpayers with the highest incomes and more than 25 percent of the tax-cut benefits would go to the wealthiest one percent of the population.[31]

As taxes on the very wealthy were cut, national defense spending has remained high, largely due to the cost of the Iraq War. Beginning with a budget surplus in 2000, the cumulative deficits are projected to total over $5 trillion by 2010.[32] Such high levels of national debt make us dependent on and vulnerable to foreign countries like Japan and China to finance our trade and federal deficits. The funding of social programs for human needs and education are being slashed due to the huge deficits resulting from the tax breaks for the rich and the increased defense spending. The federal budget for fiscal year 2006 cuts funds for Medicaid, food stamps, education, transportation, health care for veterans, law enforcement, medical research, and safety inspections for food and drugs. It also contains big new tax cuts for the wealthy. The implicit rationale is that because we have shown such economic generosity to those at the top of the socioeconomic scale, we can no longer afford to take care of the needs of persons at the bottom of the socioeconomic scale. Congress seems to be more concerned about protecting the colossal wealth accumulated by the very top of the economic echelon than providing for the needs of the hungry, homeless and sick.

Long-term studies of wealth in the United States indicate that there have always been economic elite that owned and controlled most of the nation's resources. What have characterized the last two decades have been the increasing inequalities far beyond what could be considered fair and just according to historical standards. The level of greed at the top is approaching the limit of what a democracy can tolerate. There is a danger that the people most affected by economic hardship at the bottom of the economic ladder are becoming increasingly disaffected.

*Global Inequality*

We live in a world with a wide chasm between abundance and scarcity. According to the World Bank, there are over one billion people living on less than one dollar a day, and nearly three billion people (half of the world's population) living on less than two dollars a day. According to the United Nations Children's Fund (UNICEF) more than half the world's children, about one billion, are suffering extreme effects of poverty, war, and HIV/Aids, denying them a healthy and safe childhood. Although there is poverty in every country, most of the world's poor live in South Asia, East Asia, and sub-Saharan Africa. Living conditions for these 1.2 billion persons (the bottom 25 percent of the world's population) involve serious deprivations: the lack of adequate nutrition, safe drinking water, adequate shelter, medical care, and education. Furthermore, the increasing external debt that has accumulated in the Third World during the last two decades has resulted in a net flow ("trickle up") of capital from some of these poor developing countries to the developed countries.

Alleviating poverty will be a greater challenge as the world's population continues to increase. World population, now over 6 billion, will increase by about 100 million people per year, totaling over 9 billion by the year 2050. Ninety percent of this increase will occur in developing countries, especially in the regions with the highest incidence of poverty. Of course the story is more than merely statistics. These disparate trends are only too dramatically depicted in the faces of those suffering from starvation and war. According to The United Nations Children's Fund, over 10 million children under the age of five are dying annually from malnutrition and hunger-related diseases.

Given recurrent recessions in the developed countries, the prospects are not good that simply relying on the expected growth and trade-related expansion of the international economy will alleviate the incidence of poverty, especially in the poorest countries. Specific policies, which target objectives to help people living in abject poverty, will be necessary to avert the most extreme catastrophes as witnessed in recent years in several countries in Africa.

In 1980 a group of experts known as the Brandt Commission issued a report that was ominously predictive of the human suffering we have witnessed since:

> The problem is to reduce the demand for weapons so that resources for development can be captured before they become armaments . . . The political problems of achieving a shift are not easy to resolve. Internal politics are interwoven with military-industrial connections that influence domestic and foreign policies, arms production and arms sales abroad.[33]

At about the same time as the Brandt Commission study, two economists, M. Jegen and C. Wilbur, using World Bank data estimated the level of investment that would be required to eliminate the conditions of poverty for the poorest one-fifth of the world's population. They concluded that if world military expenditures could be reduced by only five percent per year, that sum invested yearly to promote nutrition, housing, clean water, medical services, and schooling, could greatly reduce the most abject poverty within two decades.[34]

The concept of reducing global military expenditures and investing more in human needs and economic development in the Third World is a moral and compassionate course of action. The United Nations' Millennium Development goals aim to improve the prospects for human development by 2015. These goals could be achieved at an annual cost of $40-70 billion.

In June of 2005, in a renewed spirit of concern for the poorest of the poor, the finance ministers from the Group of Eight (G8) industrialized nations (Britain, Germany, France, Italy, Canada, Japan, Russia, and the United States) agreed to cancel at least $40 billion worth of debt owed by 18 of the world's poorest nations. The goal is for the poor countries to use the money they save on debt for health care, education, and the relief of poverty. As many as 38 countries could benefit if they all meet strict targets for good governance and combating corruption, leading to a total debt relief package of more than $55 billion. The deal involves the commitment of the rich nations to provide the present value of the loan principle, $16.7 billion, to the World Bank and the African Development Bank to compensate for those assets being written off and ensures that future aid packages would not be affected. The non-governmental (N.G.O.) Jubilee Debt Campaign has called for further action to cancel 100 percent of the debt of at least 62 countries so they can meet the U.N. Millennium Development Goals of reducing poverty, hunger, and disease by 2015. Prime Minister Tony Blair of Great Britain has challenged the G8 leaders to boost international development aid by $50 billion a year. The United States allocates only $15 billion per year in foreign development assistance, or less than 0.14 percent of our GDP. France contributes about 0.4 percent of its GDP for bilateral and multilateral international assistance. The United Kingdom, Canada, and Germany contribute 0.3 percent of their GDP.[35]

The goal of significantly augmenting the investment in human needs in the Third World seems feasible if military spending could be reduced by five percent with this amount added to what is currently being spent on economic development in developing countries. It is regrettable that the United States has not embraced the moral cause of helping "the least of these" (Matthew 25:45). Instead, the record shows just the opposite. With living conditions stagnating for the over one billion persons in the world living in poverty, the United States government has chosen to spend hundreds of billions of dollars waging another war in Iraq. If just some of this extraordinary expenditure on military armaments had been invested in development projects, it would have gone a long way towards alleviating poverty among the poorest of the poor. In 2004 the military expenditures worldwide totaled $1 trillion with the United States accounting for over $400 billion, or 40 percent of the world total.

Lasting world peace will not be won by military might. What is needed are sustained committed efforts by the United States and other developed nations to overcome the poverty, disease, and misery in the Third World nations. While it is true that terrorism against the United States and other economically advanced countries has been driven by a political ideology, the abject poverty and desperate conditions of life in poor countries have proved to be fertile nurturing and recruitment ground for terrorism. The miserable conditions of life also spawn seething resentment for the rich nations who so overtly and ostentatiously flaunt their excesses through the Western dominated media, thereby fueling the fires of enmity and conflict.

*Enough for All*

There are two competing points of view concerning the world's resources: 1) There's not enough; and 2) There are sufficient resources to sustain all of life in God's Creation. Biblical scholar Walter Brueggemann refers to the modern myth of scarcity as "The Nike Story." According to the Nike Story, whoever has the most shoes, SUVs, and other luxury "toys" when he dies, wins. We end up with only what we can appropriate or commandeer for ourselves. "The story ends in despair. It gives us our present state of anxiety, fear, greed, brutality . . . It tells us not to care about anyone but ourselves—and it is the prevailing creed of American society."[36]

From Brueggemann's perspective, the Bible reveals an alternative to the Nike Story—the abundance of God. According to this biblical interpretation there is enough to go around so long as each of us takes only what each person needs. In fact, there will be even more than enough, with some left over. From the first chapter of Genesis, God not only initiates abundance (calling forth plants and fish and birds and animals) but promises continued abundance by commanding them to "increase and multiply" (Genesis 1:22). God's generosity reaches its completion on the sixth day, when God declares all this "very good" (Genesis 1:30-31). Having provided more than enough to sustain God's creation, God proclaims the seventh day a day of rest.

God blesses Abraham and Sarah and their family. God tells them to be a blessing, to bless the people of all nations. This theme of blessing continues in Genesis until the 47th chapter. In that chapter Pharaoh dreams that there will be famine in the land. So he schemes to corner, control, and monopolize the food supply. Pharaoh, in order to defend against the perceived threat of famine, introduces the principle of scarcity into the world economy by hoarding all he can get. Out of this human-made scarcity the people of Israel became so indebted to Pharaoh that they became enslaved through the "free-market" greed of Pharaoh.[37]

After centuries when Israel is liberated in the Exodus from Pharaoh's slavery, God provides for them. In the Exodus, God intervened decisively to rescue the Israelites from economic oppression and destitution. But freedom can be frightening. True to human nature it isn't long before what they have left behind starts to look better than the uncertainty and unknown that they must now face—a desert, a place of scarcity, with no apparent life-support systems. Then into the midst of their fears, fine, flaky bread suddenly materializes. This generous gift from God, *manna*, overturns their fears and anxiety about hunger. What they thought was a place of scarcity turns out to be a place of wondrous abundance.

The story of God's abundance continues into the Christian scriptures. When John the Baptist and Jesus called people to repent it had a real world application. To the question, "What then shall we do?" John gives some good answers. "Whoever has two coats must share with anyone who has none; and whoever has food must do likewise" (Luke 3: 11). If some people have too much and others have too little, the answer from the Bible is that nobody should have too much and nobody should have too little. Everyone should have enough.

It challenges the idea that we should strive to continually accumulate, and invest our time and energy into making ourselves happy, satiated, and secure. Instead, says the Baptizer, we should strive for justice and peace among all people and put our money into kingdom investments. John's message is social responsibility: clothing and food are to be shared with those in need; taxes are not to be expropriated from the peasants to finance the greed of the authorities; and the military must stop their oppression of the poor.

Jesus was born and grew up under the oppression and exploitation of the Roman Empire. In this unjust world the rich and powerful despised the poor and disadvantaged and contrived to preserve the chasm between them. Yet this was not the way things were meant to be. Jesus taught a great deal about the kingdom of God—and what he means by that is a community of mutual interdependence and support. Everywhere Jesus goes he transforms and rebalances the gap between God's abundance and human need: the blind receive their sight, the lame walk, the lepers are cleansed, the deaf hear, the dead are raised, and the poor are freed from debt.[38]

Jesus' feeding of the multitudes is an example of the new world coming into being through God. When the disciples, charged with feeding the hungry crowd, found a child with five loaves and two fish, Jesus took, blessed, broke and gave the bread. In this, Jesus demonstrated that the world is filled with abundance—enough for all. If bread is broken and shared, there will be enough for all. Jesus is engaged in repairing the social fabric and rebuilding community life.

Which is true? Pharaoh's and the Nike Story or the miraculous biblical account of God's abundance? What if we are the link between the Creator's generosity and our neighbor's need? If God's abundance is real, and scarcity only a myth, then the question of "What are we to do?" is a question about how we are to manage and rearrange God's abundance. Jesus' teachings, the story of the Exodus, and the writings of the prophets all agree: every member of society is valued by God and therefore has a stake and share in the social system.

*How To Manage A Surplus?*

Jesus' parable in Luke 12: 13-21 illustrates the potential of evil that can ensnare a person who puts wealth to the wrong uses. The wealthy farmer receives a windfall harvest—not by his own efforts; but rather, the extraordinary surplus is God's miracle. Although the man does not understand it, the real question is, "What do I do with what I have not earned, nor do I need?" Or simply, "What do I do with my surplus?"[39]

In a traditional village people live in tightly knit extended families. Anyone who has surplus is expected to provide for those in need—such were the social interrelationships upon which the survival of the whole village depended. The man in this parable has set himself apart from the mainstream of village life. Perhaps he lives in the big house on the hill, his sanctuary and prison. In his self-preoccupation and self-imposed isolation there is no one else for him to talk with, so he can only speak to himself. Has the man stored the surplus for the village's benefit? Not so, as we learn, the man intends to store up wealth, for his own comfort and pleasure. He mismanages God's surplus.

Before the man can implement his selfish scheme, God intervenes, announcing that very night he will die. The story concludes with God's question left hanging in the air, "whose will all these things be?" The implication is that God's miraculous surplus will now be used for those for whom it was originally intended. The abundant life is to be found not in stockpiling for oneself, but in gathering up riches for God, and God's purposes—"loving your neighbor as yourself." How do we manage God's often miraculous and generous gifts? Just as God has supplied the gifts of soil, seeds, sun, and rain to the farmers—out of which they add their efforts to bring forth a harvest—so are all human talents and abilities gifts from God. Everything we have, then, is not so much "ours"—rather, it is what God loans to us. The harvest/surplus is never even and equal everywhere. Some places have surpluses, other places have droughts. That's why the distribution of God's miracles is left to humans to work out according to God's will on "earth as it is in heaven." The surpluses are to be managed for the good of all God's children—everyone in God's global commonwealth.

*What and Whose Surplus?*

The dictionary defines synergism as: "The simultaneous actions of separate agencies, together, have greater total effect than the sum of their individual effects."[40] Such synergistic effects within the workings of our economic system have resulted in economic success for over 200 years. The problem seems to be that the system functions in a way in which some are able to appropriate greater returns from this synergism than others. All humans are copartners in the Creator's bounteous creation. While most citizens in some way participate in our productive national economy, some benefit disproportionately more than others.

There is an overall surplus generated from our economic system. Surplus accrues as that portion of the nation's total economic production of goods and services created in a given period of time, and not consumed by its citizens, nor used for replacing the capital equipment used in its production. This surplus accrues as some combination of corporate profits, personal savings, net investment, and may accrue as local, state, and federal government budget surpluses. This total net surplus is produced as a result of the synergism of all the persons participating in some substantive way in the economy. Where the surplus accumulates is, to a large degree, the result of economic policies, i.e., tax and interest rates, government expenditures and subsidies.

Are the world's wealthiest individuals like Bill Gates and the late Sam Walton "self-made" men? Did they create their own fortunes single-handedly? What about the people who work for them? Could these wealthy scions have accumulated their wealth without help? What about the school system that provided educated workers to Gates and Walton? Do they not have an obligation to pay back society for the benefits they have received from society? What about the things that provided for an orderly and civil society such as roads and highways, electric power, communications, police and fire protection? Without all these contributing factors, not the least of which is all the employees who work for them, Gates and Walton could not enjoy the extraordinary benefits of a civil society conducive to making a Pharaoh's fortune. Fairness, therefore, requires that those who have benefited the most from society should be expected to make the greatest contribution toward the common good. Although Gates' has endowed his charitable foundation to $28 billion and the foundation has given away almost $8 billion, still Gates is the world's wealthiest person with a fortune estimated at $40 billion. (To his credit Gates has said, as has other wealthy individuals, that he doesn't need the recent hefty tax cuts for the wealthy.)

The concept of fairness is that people are obligated to give back in proportion to which they have received. Tom Chappell of Tom's Toothpaste believes that corporations have a social role to play. In his 1993 book, *The Soul of Business: Managing for Profit and the Common Good,* he writes, "The ultimate goal of business is not profit. Profit is merely a means toward the ultimate aim of affirming the health and dignity of human beings . . . and affirming the health of the environment—the common good." Tom's Corporation gives away a hefty 10 percent of its pretax profits to charities, when by relative standards less than two percent is considered generous. The company offers its employees three months of paid maternity leave, provides childcare subsidies and encourages workers to spend five percent of their paid work time doing volunteer service. The growth of such socially responsible companies as Ben and Jerry's, The Body Shop, Stonyfield Farm, and Working Assets demonstrates that consumers can be attracted to products and companies that promote the public good.

The concept of fairness is that people are obligated to give back in proportion to what they have received. In the United States charitable contributions totaled about $241 million in 2003, or 2.2 percent of GDP, according to the American Association of Fundraising Counsel. Part of the stated rationale for tax cuts that favored the wealthy was the expectation that the cuts would induce greater charitable giving. This has not happened. Despite hefty tax breaks for the wealthiest individuals, charitable giving has declined. While 90 percent of those with annual incomes above $200,000 make charitable contributions, these high earners gave just 3.4 percent of their incomes in 2003, down from 3.7 percent in 2000. Yet the low-income earners, who actually made charitable contributions, donated a whopping 26 percent of their incomes.[41] It does not seem to be the trend that voluntary, charitable giving will be able to bridge the gap between increasing human needs and diminished federal, state, and local revenue. The concept of progressive taxation is based on the principal of fairness that those who have gained the most by the workings of the system and their position in it ought to return the greatest contribution of support.

*The Politics of Greed*

Many of the trends over the last several decades have run contrary to these more generous examples of human response to God's abundance. More scandalous than the increase in poverty and homelessness, more grievous than the squandering of the trillions dollars of a cumulative budget surplus, or raiding of the Social Security trust fund—by far the greatest travesty by our public officials has been to sell into bondage our children and grandchildren who will be burdened with paying off trillions of dollars of debt from now to eternity. As indicated previously, the unwarranted tax cuts for high-income and wealthy citizens have aggravated the federal budget deficit, along with the unnecessary and misguided war in Iraq. At the same time, we face real needs: improving and rebuilding our crumbling infrastructure of bridges and highways, improving health and education, environmental clean up, and shoring up Social Security and Medicare. (At the time this book went to press, the recovery costs from hurricanes Katrina and Rita, which devastated the Gulf Coast, were estimated to total over $200 billion.)

How we manage a productive economy that produces large surpluses needs much rethinking, especially in the wake of the recent cases exposing corporate fraud such as the Enron scandal. Should the surplus remain with those who have benefited most from the economic system (promoted by the Bush Administration's huge tax cuts for the wealthiest individuals), *or* should the priority be to provide for unmet basic human needs in this country and beyond?

# 6

## MYTH #4: MORE-IS-BETTER VERSUS THE QUALITY OF LIFE

Economic growth, technically defined as the increase in the gross domestic product (GDP), the measure of the market value of all goods and services produced by a country in one year, also results in diseconomies, or costs incurred to society as a result of economic growth. As communities grow, congestion of roads and transportation systems means commuters pay a higher cost in time spent commuting. Higher levels of economic activity mean higher levels of pollution that result in higher health costs due to a higher incidence of respiratory illness and diseases.

Ethicist John B. Cobb, Jr. along with economist Herman Daly devised a carefully computed "Index of Sustainable Economic Welfare."[42] The index is based on the notion that measures of national economic output are not the best way to measure social and economic welfare. The measure of GDP fails to exclude negative costs such as pollution, crime, environmental damage, and the costs of congestion and automobile gridlock. According to their analysis,

> We are exhausting resources and polluting our world. These costs of growth now equal the gains. Individual pursuits of wealth no longer increase the real wealth of the community as a whole. Typically it concentrates wealth in a few hands while imposing costs on the whole society.[43]

Likewise, the recent "jobless recovery" from the 2001-2003 recession indicates that the economy can grow while excluding millions from the gains of economic expansion.

Considering the environmental devastation resulting from the high consumption levels in the developed world, the present scale of the world economy is ecologically unsustainable. The Earth's natural resources cannot sustain the high levels of resource consumption and pollution so exemplified in the United States. However, given that three-fourths of the world's people are poor and aspire to higher standards of living, and since it is extremely doubtful that the affluent fourth are prepared to cut their consumption drastically in order to share with those who have more urgent needs, then it seems the world is destined to increase industrial production greatly in order to respond to these increasing needs. The enormous challenge is to strike a healthy balance between economic expansion and the resultant negative environmental impacts. Given the low standard of living in half of the world's population, and considering the problems caused by excess in the industrial countries (from air pollution to obesity), it could be said that those of us in the developed world are suffering from "over consumption." Jesus warned about the problems of excess: "Do not keep striving for what you are to eat and what you are to drink, and do not keep worrying. For it is the nations of the world that strive after all these things, and your Father knows that you need them. Instead, strive for his kingdom, and these things will be given to you as well" (Luke 12 29-31).

The word *development* in reference to poor, Third World (formerly referred to as "less-developed countries") has become somewhat suspect over the last several decades. The usual usage of the term "development" refers largely to the increase in the productive capacity of a country, and the measure of economic growth is used as one of the main indicators. Often economic expansion in poor countries has been at the direction and benefit of advanced industrial countries. The infamous history of colonialism, which exploited the natural resources of the indigenous peoples, was for the economic benefit of advanced economies. The result in these economies has often been "dualistic,"—an elite aligned with the interests of foreign investors and corporations has prospered while the great majority of the population has continued to live in abject poverty. Unfortunately, this kind of economic development has not been accompanied by political and social development. Indeed there were instances where political developments were sabotaged by developed countries that felt their own economic interests would better be served by dictators rather than democracies. Clandestine policies and operatives of the United States participated in the overthrow of democratically elected governments in Iran in 1953, in Guatemala in 1954, and had an instrumental role in the coup in Chile in 1973, to name only a few.

Critics of "development" argue that the economic relations between the industrialized nations and the poorer Third World nations have resulted in the "dependency" of the poor economies on the developed nations. The dilemma is well articulated by Daley and Cobb in *For the Common Good*:

> There can be no effective national economy if people cannot feed themselves and otherwise meet their essential needs. Hence a national economy for [the whole] community will be a relatively self-sufficient economy. This does not preclude trade, but it does preclude *dependence* on trade, especially where the nation cannot participate in determining the terms of trade [relative prices of exports to imports].
>
> There is, of course, no assurance that a national economy will serve the interests of its people. It may serve the interests of a small ruling class and exploit the people. We do not believe that any system will guarantee justice and righteousness. Nevertheless, there is more possibility for people to participate in the decisions of their own national government than those of another one or of a transnational corporation. In some instances the national-state may be too small a level at which to seek relative self-sufficiency . . . The main formal point is that a political community cannot be healthy if it cannot exercise a significant measure of control over its economic life.[44]

No wonder there has been a disconnect between economic growth in poorer countries and the lack of progress in the living standards of most of their population. For example, in several countries in recent years development projects included building large dams to generate hydroelectricity for export industries. The dams, however, also resulted in the flooding of villages. So as the overall economy increased, few would share in the profits of the multinational companies, but a far greater number of citizens were further impoverished. Without a political system to address these inequities—the condition of widespread impoverishment will continue.

Within our country and globally, the quality of life including the extension of human and civil liberties now must be considered in tandem and integral to the discussion of economic growth. Only if the quality of life of the entire global community is improving, not declining, could the terms "growth" and "development" have any real meaning.

# 7

# MYTH #5: DETERMINISM VERSUS GOD'S AMAZING GRACE

From the earliest times, stories of good and evil, like the stories of the ancient Greek authors, have had strong appeal. Homer, for example, wrote about the heroic adventures of Ulysses. More recently modern epics like *Star Wars, Harry Potter,* and *The Lord of the Rings* continue to suggest the strong appeal of stories of good versus evil. It also seems that in response to the terrible events of 9/11, the rhetoric of good versus evil has intensified.

The roots of this theme of good and evil are found in the history of ancient religions. In Persia, 700 years before Christ, the prophet Zoroaster taught of the universal struggle of good eventually triumphing over evil. This teaching very likely influenced the development of Judeo-Christian and Islamic thought. In terms of this polarized way of thinking, the clash of good and evil (with no middle shades), only results in calamity destruction, and annihilation.

Mythology and history, however, present us with an alternative story of reconciliation and redemption. The *transformation* story is the alternative to the story of cataclysmic battle between good and evil. Film reviewers have pointed out the classic story of "Beauty and the Beast" was revised into the more modern version, *Shrek.* This kind of story, focusing on the possibility of change, recounts in this case the redemption of the monster, his conversion, accomplished by Beauty's courage, perseverance, and enduring commitment.

People tend to also interpret the Bible according to these two kinds of stories. Some read the Bible as a battle between good and evil, with good triumphing after the apocalyptic battles and catastrophes that are interpreted literally from the book of Revelation. The other way of reading the Bible is to see it as a way that God is attempting to reconcile and redeem a broken and wayward world: this is a story of *transformation*—the future is open, and God is willing to work with and through humans to heal and restore a broken world.

Thus, these two predominant views of interpreting the Bible have different things to say about the future. One is of a battle between good and evil that will result in an inescapable catastrophic end of the world. Only those who are in God's good graces will be saved, and the rest will be "left behind." This view has abandoned hope for the survival of the earth and waits in resigned disillusionment for the end to come. It was voices from this camp that tried to cast the horrendous events of 9/11 as fitting into their apocalyptic view of the "last days."

The remarkably popular *Left Behind* series of novels represent the former (catastrophic) view of the end of the world. The series is co-authored by Tim LaHaye a member of the religious right wing with an agenda. LaHaye joined with Jerry Falwell to found the "Moral Majority" in 1979, and has continued to promote a conservative political agenda.

Hal Lindsey's *The Late Great Planet Earth* preceded the *Left Behind* novels some 30 years earlier. The public's fascination with the end-of-the-world predictions go back to the 1830s when John Darby came over from England with some new theories about how the world will end. Ever since there have been those in line with Darby, Lindsey, and LaHaye who try to force-fit current events through this end-times template. That is, the view put forth, widely rejected by most biblical scholars, is a kind of fatalism for the future and a view that everything is destined to get worse and worse. The *Left Behind* series promotes fear mongering about the threat of big government and a conspiracy of an elite who are actively at work to create a one-world socialist state. This perspective leads to a sense of despair and discouragement. Why work for social change if everything is hopelessly destined to get worse? Why be concerned about the environment if Jesus is coming back soon? So presumably there is a kind of use-it-before-you-lose-it mentality among those who literally interpret the end-times references in the book of Revelation.

Fortunately, there is another view of biblical prophecy based on a different biblical interpretation that the future is open, undetermined and capable of being redeemed if people change their behavior in time. The prophets in the Hebrew Bible (Old Testament) share this view that catastrophe need not happen, if people change their ways and realign with God. This view is courageously hopeful. It is also the hope we have in the life and teaching of Jesus—and his prayer that "thy kingdom come and thy will be done *on earth* as it is in heaven." Jesus' new realm of God was a master plan for the transformation of our planet—not for escaping to some ethereal other time and place. And as for the end of time, let us remember Jesus' words, "But about that day and hour no one knows. Neither the angels of heaven, nor the Son, but only the Father" (Matthew 24:26). Instead of the *Left Behind* view of escape and disengagement, the more hopeful biblical vision is that people can be part of the in-breaking of God's new realm here and now to transform our present world into something far healthier and better for all. Unfortunately, this open-ended view does not receive equal time in the conservatively biased corporate media.

New Testament scholar Walter Wink points out that "the destruction of the World Trade Center," and other targets "was not an apocalypse or end of the world." Although the problems associated with terrorism are a new reality in our lives, this is not the End of the World. There are more threatening conditions that could result in the End, such as global warming, the hole in the ozone layer, overpopulation, starvation and malnutrition, the destruction of species and the rain forests, pollution of the water and air, pesticide and herbicide poisoning, erosion of topsoil, over fishing, and the continuing possibility of a nuclear mishap. Says Wink, we are "witnessing the greatest annihilation of species in the last 65 million years, and our children may live to witness ecocide with their own eyes."[45] Is an environmental catastrophe our "fate," or can we repent our profligate ways and avoid a possible calamity?

This book is written from a transformation perspective—a view of being open to the possibilities and potential of the future—and opposes the point of view of economic determinism and causality inherent in the theory of the free-market economy. In our world today, the "free-market" economic ideology is associated with political persuasions that apparently require high degrees of control and secrecy. For example the Patriot Act (and more extreme subsequent proposed version Patriot Act II), the secrecy now revealed that went into staging of the war against Iraq, and the secrecy surrounding Vice-President Cheney's refusal to reveal which executives from what energy companies he met with in preparing the administration's energy policy, all have occurred in a political atmosphere that strongly advocates the free-market economic model.

In this regard, some observations by political scientist Karl Deutsch, a pioneer in systems thinking are relevant. According to Deutsch, a system's lack of openness to its environment, and its rigidity and inability to learn, respond, and change to new information and situations are systemic pathologies and, as such, jeopardize the system's survival. In his classic book, *The Nerves of Government,* Deutsch turned to concepts from philosophy and religion when he wrote about what would protect a system from various such system pathologies. According to Deutsch:

> All system failures involved the overvaluation of the near over the far, the familiar over the new, the past over the present, and the present over the future. They involved overestimation of the organization compared to its environment, of its past commitments over new ones, and of its current will and inner structure over all possibilities of fundamental change. [46]

Deutsch says that the anecdote to these system failures is *humility*. The attitude of humility is one of openness to information outside of oneself, to experiences as well as to criticism, and to the needs of others. Humility also is characterized by a skeptical attitude toward one's own ability. How does our nation's economic and political system rank on the scale of humility?

Another system protection to maintain system health is *grace*. According to Deutsch grace is "information or events originating from outside ourselves as answers to our innermost problems."[47] Grace thus implies attitudes of openness and an orientation to the world beyond ourselves; the expectation that the universe does in fact contain the essential information and resources that may be necessary for the solution to problems but are missing from our present circumstances; and readiness and receptivity toward new experiences and new events.

Deutsch quotes the biblical text, "You shall love your neighbor as yourself" (Matthew 22:39) in prescribing *love* as a value that orients a system to openness rather than rigidity and closure. To achieve peace in a warring world we need greater openness to overcome the human defensive tendency to divide humankind into "us" and "them" groups. Erik Erikson in his classic essay on Ingmar Bergmann's *Wild Strawberries* writes about the pageantry and ritual of national and patriotic ceremonies referring to them as "a heritage of both triumph and of deadly danger for human adulthood."[48] Humankind is divided into "national, ideological, or religious bodies that consider their own kind the model image of mankind as fully intended in their version of creation and history, for the survival of which they are ready to kill as well as to die . . . At the same time, we must acknowledge a universal goal in mankind which has, over the millennia, led to larger and larger units of an ever more inclusive identity."[49]

Erikson writes that this group identity "can bring about the truest, and the best in loyalty and cooperation, heroism and inventiveness, while committing different human 'kinds' to a history of reciprocal enmity and destruction on an increasingly species-wide scale . . . And we must learn . . . how virtues such as Love and Care, in turn, contribute to a more insightful and universal *ethics*."[50] According to Erikson, the purpose of the great religions and philosophies is to counteract the divisive potential inherent in human nature that rejects persons who are perceived to be different than our own self-identified group. "Such 'sinful' tendencies as exclusivity or rejectivity thus were counteracted, say, in the Christian world view by the universal concepts of *Agape* [universal love] and *Caritas* [care-giving]."[51] The health and survival of society is dependent on the expressions of counter-cultural values that challenge the status quo. Without that challenge the social structures will become rigid, ossified, and inadaptable to a changing world. In a world stock-piled with nuclear weapons we cannot afford the potential of projecting onto "others" our hidden selves we are rejecting.

Preaching and teaching biblically is advocacy for the values of humility, grace, love, and the hope that the future is open to redemption and transformation—all values counter to the prevalent closed-ended, control-oriented political and economic values of our times. History is not fixed; humans are not fated for a predetermined end. Through God's amazing grace the future is open, all things are possible, and God invites us to be open to God's transformation working through us.

# 8

# MYTH #6: PRIVATIZATION VERSUS STEWARDSHIP

The ascendancy of religious fundamentalism over the last several decades has coincided with a new assertion of an ideological conservatism and "free-market" economic policies. The religious emphasis on personal salvation has coincided with the emphasis on economic "privatization," now including the proposal to shift Social Security from its intended purpose of social insurance to a system of private retirement accounts. The biblical view gives a theologically different perspective.

*Social Resonsibility*

Stewardship is the English word chosen to translate the Greek word in the New Testament, *oikonomia*, from which we get the word economics. The basic meaning of the Greek word *oikonomia* is "management of a household." Stewardship and economics then are closely related in meaning. John Reumann has shown that the biblical concept of stewardship (*oikonomia*) evolved in ancient times from terminology referring to managing a single household to the largest "household" imaginable, that of the world or universe. This extension of meaning followed a logical progression from household to city to the entire universe. Just as in a household there must be a household manager, God's household management involved the world including the affairs of human beings.[52]

So in biblical terms God is also a steward, for God not only created but also manages the entire cosmic household. It is this broad, cosmic perspective of the term stewardship that the Apostle Paul uses in his letter to the Ephesians. Paul speaks of a cosmic "plan for the fullness of time" (Ephesians 1:10) by which God, as chief steward, manages all of creation. God the Creator worked from a master design and plan. God created a paradise on earth. When God calls upon the human to take care of the garden and "to till it and keep it" (Genesis 2:15), we should think of earth-keeping rather than dominance and exploitation. God has called us to be agents of stewardship (maintaining and protecting) in all areas of God's Creation.

As discussed earlier, perhaps the key word is *responsibility*. Responsibility literally means to be able to respond. God calls us to a stewardship of caring and responsibility for all aspects of life. Just as we are to take care of the physical environment, so we are also responsible for our social environment that is affected by how just is the distribution of our God-given resources.

Likewise we are to be held accountable not only for our own actions, or lack of action, but for those of our country as well. One of the great theologians of the last century, Reinhold Niebuhr, reminded us that we could not only view sin as individual and a matter of personal conscience. Rather, there is social sin, sin that is not the result of individual choice—but results from the ways society functions. Few of us would have consciously chosen for there to be a quantum leap in the numbers of homeless and hungry, resulting from a sinful misallocation of resources. The same system that works so well to reward the majority of people also seems to exclude some from the benefits and prosperity that most of us enjoy.[53]

Responding to the needs of the hungry and homeless is not just a matter of individual conscious, charity and actions. All the personal charity will not be enough to solve the serious problems that are threatening to tear apart the cohesion of the social fabric that has held our nation together for over two centuries. Individuals cannot, with charity, fill the gap that was created when the government abandoned its role to assist those who are most disadvantaged and to integrate them into the social and economic mainstream. This book argues that the ideology of "free-market" economics has served the interests of the status quo. And the proposition that the market-based economic system will automatically solve the serious social problems of our time is false and is contradicted by orthodox economic theory itself, according to the theory of the second-best.

The Scriptures make it clear that the communities of biblical times were under obligations to treat the disadvantaged in differential ways. The most disadvantaged, who could not provide or protect themselves, were to be provided for and protected in those early communities. Their social understanding was based upon their theology and community identity. In being obedient to God's covenant responsibilities, these communities were practicing biblical ethics and in harmony with the contemporary ethical thought of philosopher John Rawls: a just society is characterized by a continuous improvement in the prospects of the least advantaged. Because of their faithful stewardship in protecting and providing for all persons, they experienced *shalom*, a state of peace and prosperity.

*Social Security: A Crisis of Misinformation.*

In spite of a prolonged media blitz and intensive Presidential crusade, the dire prophesies of the imminent bankruptcy and collapse of Social Security has been shown to be wild hyperbole. So far (by mid-2005), the public has not accepted the President's and conservative pundit's manifesto for privatizing Social Security. The alarmist misinformation about the future insolvency of the Social Security system is a smokescreen from which emerged the proposal for transferring some Social Security funds to private ("personal") accounts. Behind the smoke screen is an ideology that opposes the government's role as steward of the general well-being of its people, and at the same time advocates for government policies that favor those who are the most well-off. The debate is, again, about what kind of society America should be. The issue is divisive and exploits younger adults' fears that Social Security will not be there for them when they reach retirement age. A program that has over decades successfully provided for retirees and others in need through the participation of almost every citizen is being challenged by an appeal to personal greed over the common good of society.

President Bush has proposed a radical transformation of Social Security from a program that is intended to redistribute income from the more affluent to the retired, elderly and those in need. Social Security is part of our nation's safety net of collective social insurance and guaranteed retirement benefits. What is proposed to replace it in part, or eventually entirely, is that of a system of private accounts based on the notion of "ownership," an appeal to self-interest (everyone-out-for-themselves) as opposed to the prevailing notion of a national common good. According to these ideological crusaders, the key to this Social Security "reform" is reducing the size and changing the nature of Social Security, which now pays benefits of half a trillion a year, and which will only grow bigger as America grows older. One of its critics calls Social Security a "Titanic . . . headed toward the iceberg."

The crusade may potentially be self-fulfilling: If the public believes that Social Security is going bankrupt, Social Security will lose public support, further jeopardizing the trust fund's solvency. Roger Lowenstein, after studying the 225-page annual report of the Social Security trustees and conducting extensive interviews with actuaries and economists, concluded, "the system is probably in need of a small adjustment of the sort that congress has approved in the past."[54]

The approximately 47 million Social Security recipients include retirees and their dependents, under-age survivors of deceased workers and the disabled. The benefits are paid from a payroll tax on the earnings of current workers and their employers. The program is highly efficient with low costs and nearly universal participation. Benefits are proportional to the level of one's earnings with a tilt toward progressivism—with those at the bottom getting more in proportion to their earnings and those at the top getting less. Social Security was designed to replace 40 percent of the average retiree's previous income.

Those who had contributed at the lowest income levels receive as much as 60 percent of their former earnings, while those at the top (presently capped at $90,000) receive 30 percent of their earnings. The system also delivers another social benefit of stability and social cohesion. People know that if they contribute throughout their working lives—they are guaranteed a pension.

Currently, and for the next decade, Social Security is running a hefty surplus because the payroll tax is bringing in more dollars than what goes out in benefits. The surplus is invested in a trust fund, currently at one and a half trillion dollars. But by 2018 with the retirements of the baby boomers, it will have to draw on the assets in the trust fund in order to fully pay benefits. According to the agency's best guess, the system will exhaust its reserves in 2042. After that it could only cover about 73 percent of the scheduled benefits. Over a 75-year period the cumulative deficit would amount to $3.7 trillion. Due to the inherent uncertainty of trying to make projections so far in the future, there is a possibility that this projection is too pessimistic and that the system will continue to be solvent without need of major adjustments. In comparison, the possible $3.7 trillion deficit poses less of a threat to the government's solvency than the cost of making President Bush's first term tax cuts permanent, estimated at $11.6 trillion over the same time frame—or the Medicare prescription bill, estimated at $8.1 trillion over the 75 year time frame. (According to somewhat more optimistic projections by the Congressional Budget Office, the trust fund won't run out until 2052, and after that Social Security should cover 81 percent of proposed benefits.)

Since the government has been operating at a deficit, it has been using the surplus from the Social Security trust fund to pay its bills. This is the target of so many of its critics. They say that Social Security tempts the federal government into spending more than it should. Indeed, according to the Office of Management and Budget in the last four years, some $634 billion that was designated for the trust fund has been spent on current programs. If there is no money in the trust fund when it is needed to pay for the rising number of retirees, the government will have to borrow. This new borrowing, estimated to be between one and two percent of our country's gross product, is less than the present federal deficit of four percent of GDP (gross domestic product). If these government budget deficits continue due to the recent tax cuts and the ongoing war in Iraq, then the layering of the Social Security borrowing on top of the borrowing to cover the deficit could become burdensome on the economy.

From its very beginning in 1935, conservatives have opposed the Social Security program. Throughout the years some of its loudest critics have campaigned for a voluntary program. Since most people do not or cannot save enough for their retirement, under a voluntary system, many who opted out would wind up destitute. The higher-earning workers who receive a lower proportional benefit would most certainly opt out of the program. This is a case of adverse selection: wealthier persons who contribute the most would exit the system, thus leaving greater burden and less revenue for the poorer people who remain.

The last perceived crisis involving the solvency of the Social Security System was during the Reagan Administration. The crisis then was also overstated and alarmist. President Reagan's budget director warned against the system's imminent bankruptcy and proposed cutting benefits. The crisis was resolved when a 15-member commission proposed a compromise plan of benefits cuts and tax hikes. The payroll tax was increased from 10.16 percent to 12.4 percent, and the retirement age was raised over a phase in period from 65 to 67. The commission's intent was for the system to build a trust fund with its reserves accumulating sufficiently to see it through to the middle of the 21st century. Subsequent Social Security annual reports showed projections of solvency for 75 years.

According to Roger Lowenstein's analysis, the only thing that has changed in the outlook for Social Security is perception—based more on ideology and politics rather than economic reality. It is true that Social Security actuaries have recently produced a more pessimistic long-range projection indicating that over the next 75 years it will come up short by an average of 1.89 percent of payroll. Rather than this being a doomsday scenario as is has been politically cast, this "crisis" can be fixed with relatively modest combination of small benefit cuts and increases in taxes. The recent gloomier forecast from the Social Security Administration is based on male longevity rising from today's 82 years to 86 years by 2080, a somewhat speculative assumption regarding continuing significant medical improvements. As is true with any long-range projection, tiny swings in any of the variables could affect the outlying years more positively or negatively. The point remains that given the trust funds continuing surplus, the trust fund should continue to cover benefits for the next 75 years, or close to it.

Privatization will not, by itself, improve whatever shortfalls are projected for the future. Social Security supplies the majority of income for two-thirds of the nation's elderly. According to the Social Security agency in the year 2000, 48 percent of the elderly would have lived below the poverty line had they not been receiving Social Security. Thus any scheme that will reduce benefits could have a devastating impact on millions of retirees. This is the main risk associated with private accounts. Under the proposal, younger workers could divert a portion of their payroll taxes into individual accounts. Upon retirement, these workers would get reduced benefits, supplemented by whatever accumulations had resulted from their investments. Since the diverted funds would not be available to pay benefits to current retirees, however, the government would have to undertake significant borrowing to pay people currently receiving benefits. Critics of the plan proposed by the President, point out that the diversion of money into individual accounts would not be a savings for the government, since it would have to borrow to offset the loss of diverted dollars. Thus, the plan for individual accounts is a transfer, not a savings. Furthermore, according to the assumptions about future stock market earnings, private accounts would not fully make up for the benefits cuts necessitated by the program. Since the stock market's sharp declines over the past few years, many people are wary of gambling their retirement funds in the stock market versus a guaranteed benefit from Social Security. Private accounts have been implemented over the last few years in England and Sweden. According to widely published analyses, the results have been disappointing and are not cited in support of the privatization proposals by its proponents.

Today, Social Security benefits amount to 4.3 percent of total national income (GDP). The current, most likely, projection assumes that over the next 75 years the figure will rise to 6.6 percent. One proposal to fill any shortfall, 40 or 50 years hence, would be to now begin to gradually raise the cap on income subject to the payroll, currently at $90,000. With the distribution of income becoming more skewed toward upper-income persons, those who had enjoyed the greatest increase in earnings have escaped paying proportionally higher taxes into the Social Security fund. These are also the persons who have most benefited by the reduction in taxes on income and capital gains championed by the Bush Administration. These adjustments could be made without reducing benefits to the middle and lower income retirees who need the benefits the most. Rescinding the Bush Administration's tax cut to the wealthiest one percent of the population would also cover any future shortfall. Another proposal would freeze the estate tax in 2009, when the exemption reaches $3.5 million per person. Larger estates (about 10,000 such estates a year) could be taxed with the proceeds added to Social Security's trust fund.[55]

Therefore our nations's social responsibility to its citizens should not be undermined by misinformation that discredits a program that benefits the vast majority.

# 9

## CONCLUSIONS

This book began with the viewpoint that a cultural war was waging between the prevailing "free-market" ideology and biblical values. After all, the conclusion of this book, while not altogether different; nevertheless, is perhaps more profound. The different values expressed by the two camps go beyond different cultural values organized around competing ideologies. Rather, the two camps reflect different levels of consciousness, which manifest and promote different values.

All the world's major religions promote raising human awareness of the profounder meaning of life. The values of the world's major religions challenge humanity to raise their consciousness to higher levels commensurate with the human potential for spiritual growth and development. In this regard this book has been influenced by Dr. David Hawkins' book, *Power vs. Force: the Hidden Determinants of Human Behavior.* Although Hawkin's book is not written from any "religious" viewpoint, it is a profoundly spiritual work

In his book, Dr. Hawkins, has delineated a hierarchy of human consciousness. The book sets forth a scale of the entire human emotional and spiritual range. It is based on the science of kinesiology, the study of muscular response to stimuli or conditions. According to the medical research documented in Dr. Hawkins' book, kinesiology exposes for the first time, the intimate connection between mind and body, revealing that the whole body—not just the mind—"thinks." According to years of experiments conducted by researchers, a positive muscle reaction is produced in response to a statement that is obviously true. A negative response occurs if the test subject is presented with a false statement. Through these techniques, there is an objective basis for distinguishing truth from falsehood. There is a negative and weakening physiological response to falsehood. When we are not truthful, there is a physical price to be paid.

According to Dr. Hawkins' scale or "Map of Consciousness," the highest levels of consciousness and truth are love, joy, peace, and enlightenment. The world's great religious founders exhibited these highest levels. The lowest levels of consciousness are shame, guilt, apathy, grief, fear, desire, anger, and pride. The mid-point of the scale is courage, which according to Hawkins is the first positive spiritual and emotional level after the negative emotions at the lowest levels of consciousness.

The major contribution of Dr. Hawkins' significant book is that it clearly delineates the difference between power and force. According to Dr. Hawkins, power arises from meaning—the deepest truths about life. "Power is always associated with that which supports the significance of life itself."[56] In contrast, force is the human attempt to impose one's will upon life. Force is contrived and may be contrary to what is true, meaningful, and life enhancing. This brief summary cannot do justice to Dr. Hawkins many insights. One short example will have to suffice: In India, Gandhi used the *power* of non-violence to defeat the violent *force* of British colonial rule. Power makes humans strong; force makes humans weak. Again as we read in the Apostle Paul, "The Lord said to me, 'My grace is sufficient for you, for power is made perfect in weakness'" (2 Corinthians 12:9).

This book, in hand, was written as a challenge to encourage the advocacy of biblical values against the prevailing values of greed and covetousness foundational to "free-market" ideology. Advocating biblical values will help people realize higher levels of consciousness. A nation that is stuck on the lower emotional levels of fear and revenge associated with an unending and poorly defined war, and with an economy that values greed and unconstrained acquisitiveness, needs a raising of consciousness to values of wisdom, love, joy, peace, and enlightenment.

Why would a religious leader engage in such controversial issues as presented in this book? The answer would be found inherently in the salient issues addressed by Douglas Meeks in his work "God as Economist": 1) Unjust economic conditions contradict the biblical understanding of God and thereby destroy the true worship of God. Thus, economic injustice diminishes our spiritual life; and 2) Worshipping a distorted and misunderstood view of God and our biblical faith contributes to the dehumanization and injustices in economic life. So our diminished spiritual life further contributes to socio-economic injustice. Therefore, there is a direct, reciprocal link between our spiritual life and economic justice in the world.[57]

To preach and teach biblically will evoke the major themes of social justice, fairness, and all the values that contribute toward a world at peace. Yet, as suggested by this book, such themes are inherently counter-cultural and subversive to the predominant political and economic ideology of our times. The preacher or teacher need not have an advanced degree in economics or political science.

Just expounding the biblical texts with the integrity to the major canonical themes will be sufficient to challenge the economic false myths of our times.

The dramatic and familiar view of Earth from space is so miraculous that it has not yet become commonplace. Suspended in a lifeless, frozen or searing universe, the living Earth appears unique among ten billion trillion planets. Viewed from space, Earth appears in its gem-like wholeness.

Likewise, from God's perspective—the world's economy is one, unified, interactive system. The Spirit of God as reflected in the scriptures can give us insights into the spirit of our stewardship on earth. After reading about the ravens that neither sow nor reap, Felipe, a Nicaraguan *campesino* reflected:

> God gives things to people like he gives them to the birds, and more than to the birds. He gives the earth and all that we take out of the earth to eat and to clothe ourselves and to live in comfort. But people take things away from each other. Then some have and others don't. That's why, if we seek the kingdom of brotherhood and justice, we're going to have all the things that God gives.[58]

May those who are called to be advocates of the vision Jesus set forth as the "kingdom of God"—a new global commonwealth of peace and justice—have as much courage, wisdom, and witness to that vision as Felipe.

# APPENDIX 1

**THE EARTH CHARTER**
***Earth Charter USA*, 2100 "L" St. NW, Washington, DC, 20037**

PREAMBLE

We stand at a critical moment in Earth's history, a time when humanity must choose its future. As the world becomes increasingly interdependent and fragile, the future at once holds great peril and great promise. To move forward we must recognize that in the midst of a magnificent diversity of cultures and life forms we are one human family and one Earth community with a common destiny. We must join together to bring forth a sustainable global society founded on respect for nature, universal human rights, economic justice, and a culture of peace. Towards this end, it is imperative that we, the peoples of Earth, declare our responsibility to one another, to the greater community of life, and to future generations.

*Earth, Our Home*

Humanity is part of a vast evolving universe. Earth, our home, is alive with a unique community of life. The forces of nature make existence a demanding and uncertain adventure, but Earth has provided the conditions essential to life's evolution. The resilience of the community of life and the well-being of humanity depend upon preserving a healthy biosphere with all its ecological systems, a rich variety of plants and animals, fertile soils, pure waters, and clean air. The global environment with its finite resources is a common concern of all peoples. The protection of Earth's vitality, diversity, and beauty is a sacred trust.

*The Global Situation*

The dominant patterns of production and consumption are causing environmental devastation, the depletion of resources, and a massive extinction of species. Communities are being undermined. The benefits of development are not shared equitably and the gap between rich and poor is widening. Injustice, poverty, ignorance, and violent conflict are widespread and the cause of great suffering. An unprecedented rise in human population has overburdened ecological and social systems. The foundations of global security are threatened. These trends are perilous—but not inevitable.

*The Challenges Ahead*

The choice is ours: form a global partnership to care for Earth and one another or risk the destruction of ourselves and the diversity of life. Fundamental changes are needed in our values, institutions, and ways of living. We must realize that when basic needs have been met, human development is primarily about being more, not having more. We have the knowledge and technology to provide for all and to reduce our impacts on the environment. The emergence of a global civil society is creating new opportunities to build a democratic and humane world. Our environmental, economic, political, social, and spiritual challenges are interconnected, and together we can forge inclusive solutions.

*Universal Responsibility*

To realize these aspirations, we must decide to live with a sense of universal responsibility, identifying ourselves with the whole Earth community as well as our local communities. We are at once citizens of different nations and of one world in which the local and global are linked. Everyone shares responsibility for the present and future well-being of the human family and the larger living world. The spirit of human solidarity and kinship with all life is strengthened when we live with reverence for the mystery of being, gratitude for the gift of life, and humility regarding the human place in nature.

We urgently need a shared vision of basic values to provide an ethical foundation for the emerging world community. Therefore, together in hope we affirm the following interdependent principles for a sustainable way of life as a common standard by which the conduct of all individuals, organizations, businesses, governments, and transnational institutions is to be guided and assessed.

PRINCIPLES

I. RESPECT AND CARE FOR THE COMMUNITY OF LIFE

1. *Respect Earth and life in all its diversity.*

*a. Recognize that all beings are interdependent and every form of life has value regardless of its worth to human beings.*

*b. Affirm faith in the inherent dignity of all human beings and in the intellectual, artistic, ethical, and spiritual potential of humanity.*

2. *Care for the community of life with understanding, compassion, and love.*

*a. Accept that with the right to own, manage, and use natural resources co mes the duty to prevent environmental harm and to protect the rights of people.*

*b. Affirm that with increased freedom, knowledge, and power comes increased responsibility to promote the common good.*

3. *Build democratic societies that are just, participatory, sustainable, and peaceful.*

*a. Ensure that communities at all levels guarantee human rights and fundamental freedoms and provide everyone an opportunity to realize his or her full potential.*

*b. Promote social and economic justice, enabling all to achieve a secure and meaningful livelihood that is ecologically responsible.*

4. *Secure Earth's bounty and beauty for present and future generations.*

*a. Recognize that the freedom of action of each generation is qualified by the needs of future generations.*

*b. Transmit to future generations values, traditions, and institutions that support the long-term flourishing of Earth's human and ecological communities.*

In order to fulfill these four broad commitments, it is necessary to:

II. ECOLOGICAL INTEGRITY

5. *Protect and restore the integrity of Earth's ecological systems, with special concern for biological diversity and the natural processes that sustain life.*

*a. Adopt at all levels sustainable development plans and regulations that make environmental conservation and rehabilitation integral to all development initiatives.*

*b. Establish and safeguard viable nature and biosphere reserves, including wild lands and marine areas, to protect Earth's life support systems, maintain biodiversity, and preserve our natural heritage.*

*c. Promote the recovery of endangered species and ecosystems.*

*d. Control and eradicate non-native or genetically modified organisms harmful to native species and the environment, and prevent introduction of such harmful organisms.*

*e. Manage the use of renewable resources such as water, soil, forest products, and marine life in ways that do not exceed rates of regeneration and that protect the health of ecosystems.*

*f. Manage the extraction and use of non-renewable resources such as minerals and fossil fuels in ways that minimize depletion and cause no serious environmental damage.*

6. *Prevent harm as the best method of environmental protection and, when knowledge is limited, apply a precautionary approach.*

*a. Take action to avoid the possibility of serious or irreversible environmental harm even when scientific knowledge is incomplete or inconclusive.*

*b. Place the burden of proof on those who argue that a proposed activity will not cause significant harm, and make the responsible parties liable for environmental harm.*

*c. Ensure that decision making addresses the cumulative, long-term, indirect, long distance, and global consequences of human activities.*

*d. Prevent pollution of any part of the environment and allow no build-up of radioactive, toxic, or other hazardous substances.*

*e. Avoid military activities damaging to the environment.*

7. *Adopt patterns of production, consumption, and reproduction that safeguard Earth's regenerative capacities, human rights, and community well-being.*

*a. Reduce, reuse, and recycle the materials used in production and consumption systems, and ensure that residual waste can be assimilated by ecological systems.*

*b. Act with restraint and efficiency when using energy, and rely increasingly on renewable energy sources such as solar and wind.*

*c. Promote the development, adoption, and equitable transfer of environmentally sound technologies.*

*d. Internalize the full environmental and social costs of goods and services in the selling price, and enable consumers to identify products that meet the highest social and environmental standards.*

*e. Ensure universal access to health care that fosters reproductive health and responsible reproduction.*

*f. Adopt lifestyles that emphasize the quality of life and material sufficiency in a finite world.*

8. *Advance the study of ecological sustainability and promote the open exchange and wide application of the knowledge acquired.*

*a. Support international scientific and technical cooperation on sustainability, with special attention to the needs of developing nations.*

*b. Recognize and preserve the traditional knowledge and spiritual wisdom in all cultures that contribute to environmental protection and human well-being.*

*c. Ensure that information of vital importance to human health and environmental protection, including genetic information, remains available in the public domain.*

III. SOCIAL AND ECONOMIC JUSTICE

9. *Eradicate poverty as an ethical, social, and environmental imperative.*

*a. Guarantee the right to potable water, clean air, food security, uncontaminated soil, shelter, and safe sanitation, allocating the national and international resources required.*

*b. Empower every human being with the education and resources to secure a sustainable livelihood, and provide social security and safety nets for those who are unable to support themselves.*

*c. Recognize the ignored, protect the vulnerable, serve those who suffer, and enable them to develop their capacities and to pursue their aspirations.*

10. *Ensure that economic activities and institutions at all levels promote human development in an equitable and sustainable manner.*

*a. Promote the equitable distribution of wealth within nations and among nations.*

*b. Enhance the intellectual, financial, technical, and social resources of developing nations, and relieve them of onerous international debt.*

*c. Ensure that all trade supports sustainable resource use, environmental protection, and progressive labor standards.*

*d. Require multinational corporations and international financial organizations to act transparently in the public good, and hold them accountable for the consequences of their activities.*

11. *Affirm gender equality and equity as prerequisites to sustainable development and ensure universal access to education, health care, and economic opportunity.*

*a. Secure the human rights of women and girls and end all violence against them.*

*b. Promote the active participation of women in all aspects of economic, political, civil, social, and cultural life as full and equal partners, decision makers, leaders, and beneficiaries.*

*c. Strengthen families and ensure the safety and loving nurture of all family members.*

12. *Uphold the right of all, without discrimination, to a natural and social environment supportive of human dignity, bodily health, and spiritual well-being, with special attention to the rights of indigenous peoples and minorities.*

*a. Eliminate discrimination in all its forms, such as that based on race, col or, sex, sexual orientation, religion, language, and national, ethnic or social origin.*

*b. Affirm the right of indigenous peoples to their spirituality, knowledge, lands and resources and to their related practice of sustainable livelihoods.*

*c. Honor and support the young people of our communities, enabling them to fulfill their essential role in creating sustainable societies.*

*d. Protect and restore outstanding places of cultural and spiritual significance.*

## IV. DEMOCRACY, NONVIOLENCE, AND PEACE

13. *Strengthen democratic institutions at all levels, and provide transparency and accountability in governance, inclusive participation in decision making, and access to justice.*

*a. Uphold the right of everyone to receive clear and timely information on environmental matters and all development plans and activities which are likely to affect them or in which they have an interest.*

*b. Support local, regional and global civil society, and promote the meaningful participation of all interested individuals and organizations in decision making.*

*c. Protect the rights to freedom of opinion, expression, peaceful assembly, association, and dissent.*

*d. Institute effective and efficient access to administrative and independent judicial procedures, including remedies and redress for environmental harm and the threat of such harm.*

*e. Eliminate corruption in all public and private institutions.*

*f. Strengthen local communities, enabling them to care for their environments, and assign environmental responsibilities to the levels of government where they can be carried out most effectively.*

14. *Integrate into formal education and life-long learning the knowledge, values, and skills needed for a sustainable way of life.*

*a. Provide all, especially children and youth, with educational opportunities that empower them to contribute actively to sustainable development.*

*b. Promote the contribution of the arts and humanities as well as the sciences in sustainability education.*

*c. Enhance the role of the mass media in raising awareness of ecological and social challenges.*

*d. Recognize the importance of moral and spiritual education for sustainable living.*

15. *Treat all living beings with respect and consideration.*

*a. Prevent cruelty to animals kept in human societies and protect them from suffering.*
*b. Protect wild animals from methods of hunting, trapping, and fishing that cause extreme, prolonged, or avoidable suffering.*
*c. Avoid or eliminate to the full extent possible the taking or destruction of non-targeted species.*

16. *Promote a culture of tolerance, nonviolence, and peace.*

*a. Encourage and support mutual understanding, solidarity, and cooperation among all peoples and within and among nations.*
*b. Implement comprehensive strategies to prevent violent conflict and use collaborative problem solving to manage and resolve environmental conflicts and other disputes.*
*c. Demilitarize national security systems to the level of a non-provocative defense posture, and convert military resources to peaceful purposes, including ecological restoration.*
*d. Eliminate nuclear, biological, and toxic weapons and other weapons of mass destruction.*
*e. Ensure that the use of orbital and outer space supports environmental protection and peace.*
*f. Recognize that peace is the wholeness created by right relationships with oneself, other persons, other cultures, other life, Earth, and the larger whole of which all are a part.*

## THE WAY FORWARD

As never before in history, common destiny beckons us to seek a new beginning. Such renewal is the promise of these Earth Charter principles. To fulfill this promise, we must commit ourselves to adopt and promote the values and objectives of the Charter.

This requires a change of mind and heart. It requires a new sense of global interdependence and universal responsibility. We must imaginatively develop and apply the vision of a sustainable way of life locally, nationally, regionally, and globally. Our cultural diversity is a precious heritage and different cultures will find their own distinctive ways to realize the vision. We must deepen and expand the global dialogue that generated the Earth Charter, for we have much to learn from the ongoing collaborative search for truth and wisdom.

Life often involves tensions between important values. This can mean difficult choices. However, we must find ways to harmonize diversity with unity, the exercise of freedom with the common good, shortterm objectives with long-term goals. Every individual, family, organization, and community has a vital role to play. The arts, sciences, religions, educational institutions, media, businesses, nongovernmental organizations, and governments are all called to offer creative leadership. The partnership of government, civil society, and business is essential for effective governance.

In order to build a sustainable global community, the nations of the world must renew their commitment to the United Nations, fulfill their obligations under existing international agreements, and support the implementation of Earth Charter principles with an international legally binding instrument on environment and development.

Let ours be a time remembered for the awakening of a new reverence for life, the firm resolve to achieve sustainability, the quickening of the struggle for justice and peace, and the joyful celebration of life.

# APPENDIX 2

*Helpful Web Sites:*

| | |
|---|---|
| 1. Board of Governors of the Federal Reserve: | www.federalreserve.gov |
| 2. Center for American Progress: | www.americanprogess.org |
| 3. Center for Defense Information: | www.cdi.org |
| 4. Center on Budget and Policy Priorities: | www.cbpp.org |
| 5. Congressional Budget Office: | www.cbo.org |
| 6. Earth Charter: | www.earthcharterusa.org |
| 7. The Economist: | www.economist.org |

# ENDNOTES

1. Walter Brueggemann, *I Kings: Knox Preaching Guides*, (Atlanta: John Knox Press, 1982), 78-87.

2. Origen, “Homily on Judges 2:3.” Walter J. Burghardt, S.J., “‘Mine and Thine’ in the Early Church,” The Living Pulpit, vol. 6, no. 3 (1979): 9.

3. Robert W. Lynn, “Speaking Honestly About Money,” *Living Pulpit*, vol. 6, no. 3 (1979): 14.

4. Peter F. Drucker, *Managing the Next Century*, (New York: Truman Talley Books/St. Martin's Press, 2002), 149-50.

5. R. G. Lipsey and K. Lancaster, “The General Theory of Second-Best,” *Review of Economic Studies*, vol. 24, no. 1 (1956): 11-32. O. A. Davis and A.B. Whinston, “Welfare Economics and the Theory of the Second Best,” *Review of Economic Studies*, vol. 32, no. 1 (1965): 1-14.

6. Deirdre. McCloskey, and S. T. Ziliak, “The Standard Error of Regressions,” *Journal of Economic Literature*, vol. 34, no. 1 (1996): 97-114.

7. John F. Due, and A.F. Friedlaender, *Government Finance: Economics of the Public Sector*, (Homewood, Illinois: Irwin, 1977), 2-4.

8. Charles E. Staley, *International Economics: Analysis and Issues*, (New Jersey: Prentice-Hall, 1970), 193-194.

9. John Rawls, *A Theory of Justice*, (Cambridge: Harvard Univ. Press, 1971), 75.

10. *The Economist*, “Beyond Capitalism,” (June 12, 2004): 17.

11. Herman E. Daly & John B. Cobb, Jr., *For the Common Good: Redirecting the Economy Toward Community, the Environment, and a Sustainable Future*, (Boston: Beacon Press, 1989), 53.

12. United States Conference of Catholic Bishops, *Economic Justice for All: Pastoral Letter on Catholic Social Teaching and the U.S. Economy*, Chapter 2. A.2. (1986): www.osjspm.org.

13. Abraham Herschel, *The Prophets: An Interpretation*, vol. 1 (New York: Harper and Row, 1962), 195-220.

14. Klaus Koch, *The Prophets: The Assyrian Period*, vol. 1 (Philadelphia: Fortress Press, 1978), 60.

15. Charles Cousar, *Galatians: Interpretation Bible Commentary*, (Atlanta: John Knox Press, 1982), 62.

16. Fred Hirsch, *Social Limits to Growth*, (Cambridge: Harvard Univ. Press, 1973), 12.

17. Carlo Carretto, *Why O Lord?:The Inner Meaning of Suffering*, (Maryknoll, N.Y.: Orbis,1986) 9.

18. Timothy Ferris, *The Creation of the Universe*, (Public Broadcasting System, 1985), VHS and DVD formats.

19. Garrett Hardin, "The Tragedy of the Commons," *Science*, vol. 162 (Dec. 13, 1968): 1243-1248.

20. James Brooke, "Japan Squeezes to Get the Most of Costly Fuel," *The New York Times*, (June 4, 2005).

21. Lucy Morgan, "Moneyworld: A Special Report on State Lobbyists," *Saint Petersburg Times*, (March 7, 2004).

22. Bruce Barcott, "Changing All the Rules," *New York Times Magazine*, (April 4, 2004).

23. James K. Hammitt, "Gauging the Mercury Risk," *Los Angeles Times*, (April 16, 2005).

24. Daniel C. Maguire, *Sacred Energies: When the World's Religion Sit Down to Talk About the Future of Human Life and the Plight of this Planet*, (Minneapolis: Fortress Press, 2000).

25. Chief Seattle, Address to President Pierce, 1854.

26. *Midrash Tanchumia Kedoshim*, 8.

27. David Cay Johnson, "Richest Are Leaving Even the Rich far Behind," *The New York Times*, (June 5, 2005).

28. A.B. Kennickell, "A Rolling Tide: Changes in the Distribution of Wealth in the U.S., 1989-2001," (Washington D.C: The Federal Reserve Board, www.federalreserve.gov/pubs/oss/oss2/scindex.html).

29. M. Nord, M. Andrews, S. Carlson, *Household Food Security in the United States, 2003*, (Washington, D.C.: U.S. Department of Agriculture, ERS no. FANRR42, Oct. 2004).

30. Paul Krugman, "The Medical Money Pit," *The New York Times*, (April 15, 2005).

31. Center on Budget and Policy Priorities, "What the President's Budget Shows About the Administration's Priorities," (Washington, D.C., March 18, 2005, www.cbpp.org/2-7-05bud3htm).

32. *The Budget and Economic Outlook: An Update*, (Washington, D.C.: Congressional Budget Office, Sept. 2004).

33. W. Brandt, *North-South: A Program for Survival*, (Cambridge: MIT Press, 1980), 123-124.

34. M. E. Jegen and C. K. Wilber, *Growth with Equity: Strategies for Meeting Human Needs*, (New York: Paulist Press, 1979).

35. The Economist, *Pocket World in Figures: 2005 Edition*, (London: Profile Books Ltd., 2004), 43.

36. Walter Brueggemann, "The Liturgy of Abundance," The Christian Century, (March 24-31, 1999): 344.

37. Ibid., 342.

38. Walter Brueggemann, "Enough is Enough," The Other Side, (November-December, 2001), 12.

39. Bernard B. Scott, "How to Mismanage a Miracle," Hear Then the Para ble, (Minneapolis: Fortress Press, 1989), 127-40.

40. *Webster's New World Dictionary: Third College Edition*, (New York: Prentice Hall, 1991), 1358.

41.Daniel Altman, "Economic View; If the IRS Gets Less, Does Charity Get More?" *The New York Times,* (May 8, 2005).

42. Herman E. Daly & John B. Cobb, Jr., *For the Common Good: Redirecting the Economy Toward Community, the Environment, and a Sustainable Future*, (Boston: Beacon Press, 1989), 401-455.

43. John B. Cobb, Jr., "New Reasons for Condemning Greed," *The Living Pulpit*, vol. 12, no. 2 (2003), 9.

44. Daly & Cobb, *For the Common Good*, 173.

45. Walter Wink, "Apocalypse now?" *Christian Century*, (Oct 17, 2001), 16-19.

46. Karl W. Deutsch, *The Nerves of Government: Models of Political Communication and Control*, (New York: Free Press, 1963), 229.

47. Ibid., 230.

48. Erik H. Erikson, "Reflections on Dr. Borg's Life Cycle," *Daedalus: Adulthood*, vol. 105, no. 2 (1969), 16.

49. Ibid., 17.

50. Ibid., 17.

51. Ibid., 17.

52. John Reumann, *Stewardship and the Economy of God*, (Grand Rapids: Eerdmans, 1992), 11-24.

53. Reinhold Niebuhr, *The Nature and Destiny of Man*, vol. 1 (New York: Scribners, 1943), 246.

54. Roger Lowenstein, "A Question of Numbers," *The New York Times Magazine*, (January 16, 2005).

55. Jane Bryant Quinn, "Social Security Isn't Doomed," *Newsweek*, (March 29, 2005).

56. David R. Hawkins, *Power vs. Force: The Hidden Determinants of Human Behavior* (rev. ed), (Carlsbad: Hay House, 2002), 132.

57. Douglas Meeks, "God As Economist and the Problem of Property," *Occasional Papers, Institute for Ecumenical and Cultural Research*, (February 1984), 1.

58. Ernesto Cardenal, *The Gospel of Solentiname*, (New York: Orbis Books, 1976), 123.

## INDEX

## ABOUT THE AUTHOR

The Rev. Robert L. White currently works as a hospital chaplain. He has been a church pastor for 16 years, and served eight years as an economist with the federal government. Rev. White holds a master's degree in economics from the University of Arizona. He did additional graduate work in economics at American University and George Washington University. He also has a master's of divinity degree from Union Theological Seminary in New York City, and is an ordained minister in the National Association of Congregational Christian Churches. Rev. White currently resides in Valrico, Florida with his wife and children.